First Step in

English Discussion

1

Student Book

Iam books

Preface

First Step in English Discussion series is a basic discussion book for beginner learners. There are 12 units in series and each unit is about a different point of English speaking which is very helpful for an English-learner students. With the various exercises, interesting photos and illustrations, students will enjoy all the skills (reading, writing, listening, and speaking) and really can communicate in English, even from the beginning. This book encourages students to speak and write English accurately and fluently by providing them with a solid understanding of English language.

This book uses a simple but systematic approach (Getting Ready, Reading, Dialogue, Supper Discussion, and Language Focus) to help young learners master English speaking skills.

This series aims to motivate young learners to develop their speaking skills that will help students throughout their lives through various creative tasks such as Super Discussion and various levels of challenging questions.

First Step in English Discussion series is a useful supplement to any English language course and is suitable for both classroom teaching and self-study. The series focuses on the strong oral skills development that students need to know for basic interpersonal communication skills.

I hope many students will build language and communication skills with this *First Step in English Discussion series*. At the same time, I wish teachers will use *First Step in English Discussion series* as the most appropriate tool for teaching English as a second language.

I am convinced that through this *First Step in English Discussion series*, a lot of students will definitely have the opportunity to improve and develop their English speaking skills and abilities.

Thanks and good luck,
Lucifer EX

Contents

About This Book

step 1. Getting Ready
- This task prepares students by previewing the unit's language and ideas.
- Represent short and practical dialogs
- Key vocabulary is presented in various formats.
- The accompanying short questions ensure that students understand the topic of the Unit with colorful photos.

step 2. Reading
- This section contains a reading passage about the main topic.
- Present key vocabulary
- Develop reading skills

step 3. Building vocabulary
- Students learn vocabulary from the Reading passage.
- This vocabulary is used throughout the reading passage, so that students gradually become familiar with it.

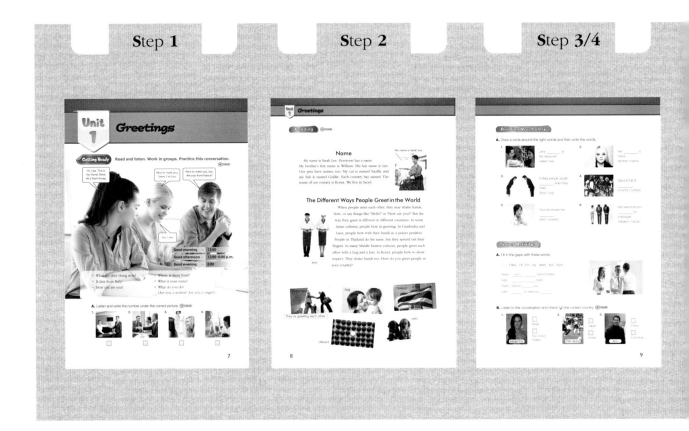

Step 1   Step 2   Step 3/4

step 4. **Super Activity!**
• Develop listening skills through targeted tasks and visual cues

step 5. **Dialog**
• Develop listening skills
• The listening task focuses on understanding the topic and related issues of the dialogue, and then focuses on detail and interpretation.

step 6. **Supper Discussion!**
• Students discuss the topic and related issues.

step 7. **Super Speaking**
• Super Speaking offers students rich opportunities to broaden and improve their speaking skills. Students work in pairs or groups and perform a variety of real-life tasks, progressing smoothly from controlled to free practice. By doing so, the amount of time students speak is increased significantly and cooperation among students is encouraged. In addition, pair and group work help students lessen their communicative stress because it is easier for them to communicate with their peers rather than their teachers.

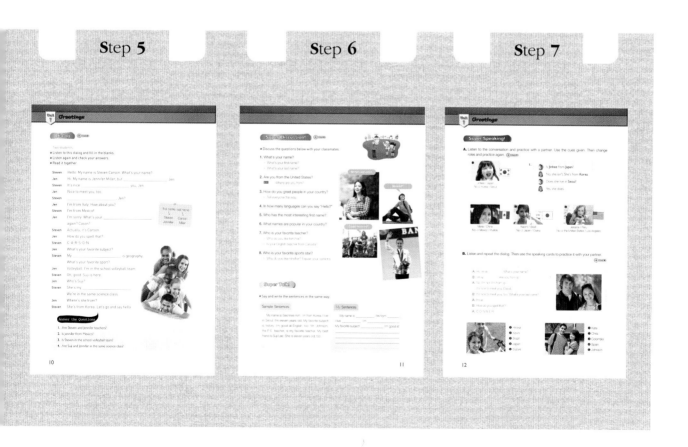

step 8. Learn & Practice

- Vivid photos and illustrations stimulate students' interest and help them understand the meaning and use of grammar. Clear and easy-to-read grammar charts present the grammar structure. The accompanying examples ensure that students understand the grammar point with colorful photos.

step 9. Exercise

- Each Learn & Practice provides various basic exercises and opportunities to practice both the forms and the uses of the grammar structure.

step 10. Super Speaking

- Super Speaking offers students rich opportunities to apply newly learned grammar to speaking activities. This section will help students to develop speaking skills. Students work in pairs or groups and perform a variety of real-life tasks, progressing smoothly from controlled to free practice.

Step 8/9   Step 10

Greetings

Getting Ready   **Read and listen. Work in groups. Practice this conversation.**

Track 1

Hi, Lisa. This is my friend Steve. He's from Korea.

Nice to meet you, Steve. I'm Lisa.

Nice to meet you, too. Are you from France?

Yes, I am.

Good morning	**12:00**
Good afternoon	**12:00–6:00 p.m.**
Good evening	**6:00**

- What are they doing now?
- Is Lisa from Italy?
- How old are you?

- Where is Steve from?
- What is your name?
- What do you do?
  (Are you a student? Are you a singer?)

A. Listen and write the number under the correct picture. Track 2

1.

2.

3.

4.

Reading ◉ Track 3

Name

My name is Sarah Lee. Everyone has a name.
My brother's first name is William. His last name is Lee.
Our pets have names, too. My cat is named Nazilla and
my fish is named Goldie. Each country has names! The
name of our country is Korea. We live in Seoul.

My name is Sarah Lee.

The Different Ways People Greet in the World

bow

When people meet each other, they may shake hands,
bow, or say things like "Hello!" or "How are you?" But the
way they greet is different in different countries. In some
Asian cultures, people bow in greeting. In Cambodia and
Laos, people bow with their hands in a prayer position.
People in Thailand do the same, but they spread out their
fingers. In many Middle Eastern cultures, people greet each
other with a hug and a kiss. In Korea, people bow to show
respect. They shake hands too. How do you greet people in
your country?

shake hands

They're greeting each other.

hug

Thailand

different

pets

8

Building Vocabulary

A. Draw a circle around the right words and then write the words.

1.

Let's _____ at the restaurant.
(meet / live)

2.

Her _____ is Olivia.
(brother / name)

3.

In Asia, people usually _____ when they meet.
(bow / hug)

4.

Seoul is full of _____.
(country / culture)

5.

God will answer her _____.
(pets / prayers)

6.

We have trust and _____ for individuals.
(respect / hands)

Super Activity!

A. Fill in the gaps with these words.

> Hello   Hi   I'm   my   meet   too   Nice

Pedro: _Hello_ , _____ name's Pedro.

Kate: _____ , _____ Kate.

Pedro: Nice to _____ you.

Kate: _____ to meet you, _____ .

B. Listen to the conversation and check (√) the correct country. ⊙ Track 4

1.

☐ Brazil

☐ the United States

Megan Fox

2.

☐ Japan

☐ Korea

Park Jisung

3.

☐ China

☐ Colombia

Jet Li

Dialog Track 5

Two students:

- Listen to this dialog and fill in the blanks.
- Listen again and check your answers.
- Read it together.

Steven	Hello. My name is Steven Carson. What's your name?
Jen	Hi. My name is Jennifer Miller, but _____ Jen.
Steven	It's nice _____ you, Jen.
Jen	Nice to meet you, too.
Steven	_____, Jen?
Jen	I'm from Italy. How about you?
Steven	I'm from Mexico!
Jen	I'm sorry. What's your _____ again? Cason?
Steven	Actually, it's Carson.
Jen	How do you spell that?
Steven	C-A-R-S-O-N.
Jen	What's your favorite subject?
Steven	My _____ is geography. What's your favorite sport?
Jen	Volleyball. I'm in the school volleyball team.
Steven	Oh, good. Suji is here.
Jen	Who's Suji?
Steven	She's my _____. We're in the same science class.
Jen	Where's she from?
Steven	She's from Korea. Let's go and say hello.

first name   last name
↓   ↓
Steven   Carson
Jennifer   Miller

Answer the Questions

1. Are Steven and Jennifer teachers?

2. Is Jennifer from Mexico?

3. Is Steven in the school volleyball team?

4. Are Suji and Jennifer in the same science class?

Super Discussion! ⦿ Track 6

• Discuss the questions below with your classmates.

1. What's your name?

    What's your first name?

    What's your last name?

2. Are you from the United States?

    No!   Where are you from?

3. How do you greet people in your country?

    Tell everyone the way.

4. In how many languages can you say "Hello?"

5. Who has the most interesting first name?

6. What names are popular in your country?

7. Who is your favorite teacher?

    Why do you like him/her?

    Is your English teacher from Canada?

8. Who is your favorite sports star?

    Why do you like him/her? Explain your opinions.

Super Talk!

• Say and write the sentences in the same way.

Sample Sentences

    My name is Seonhee Kim. I'm from Korea. I live in Seoul. I'm eleven years old. My favorite subject is history. I'm good at English, too. Mr. Johnson, the P.E. teacher, is my favorite teacher. My best friend is Suji Lee. She is eleven years old, too.

My Sentences

My name is _____. I'm from _____.
I live _____. I'm _____.
My favorite subject _____. I'm good at
_____.
_____
_____
_____

Super Speaking!

A. Listen to the conversation and practice with a partner. Use the cues given. Then change roles and practice again. ◉ Track 7

❶

Jinhee / Japan
No ⇨ Korea / Seoul

👤 Is **Jinhee** from **Japan**?

👤 No, she isn't. She's from **Korea**.

👤 Does she live in **Seoul**?

👤 Yes, she does.

②

Maria / China
No ⇨ Mexico / Puebla

③

Naomi / Brazil
No ⇨ Japan / Osaka

④

Jessica / Peru
No ⇨ the United States / Los Angeles

B. Listen and repeat the dialog. Then use the speaking cards to practice it with your partner.

◉ Track 8

A: Hi, I'm ❶ __Sarah__. What's your name?

B: I'm ❷ __David__. Are you from ❸ __the United States__?

A: No, I'm not. I'm from ❹ __Taiwan__.
   It's nice to meet you, David.

B: It's nice to meet you, too. What's your last name?

A: It's ❺ __Conner__.

B: How do you spell that?

A: C-O-N-N-E-R.

❶ Hiroka
❷ Kevin
❸ Brazil
❹ Japan
❺ Suzuki

❶ Kate
❷ Chris
❸ Colombia
❹ Spain
❺ Johnson

Learn & Practice

- There are three forms of present tense of *be*: *am*, *are*, and *is*.

- To make the negative, put *not* after *be*: *am not / are not / is not*.

- In a question, the verb *be* comes in front of the subject. **Yes/No questions** end with a question mark (?). In short answers, we add *not* if the answer is negative.

He **is** a police officer.
He **isn't** (= is not) a doctor.

She **is** a teacher.
She **isn't** (= is not) a student.

They **are** students.
They **aren't** (= are not) teachers.

Q: **Is** Kathy from Korea?
A: **Yes**, she **is**.

Q: **Are** you a pianist?
A: **No**, I'm **not**. I'm a violinist.

A. Make full sentences, positive and negative.

1. I / a student
⇨ P: I am a student.   N: I am not a student.

2. he / a singer
⇨ P: _____   N: _____

3. we / nurses
⇨ P: _____   N: _____

B. Look at the pictures and complete the sentences.

1.

Q: __Is__ she a teacher?
A: _____, _____.
　　She is a doctor.

2.

Q: _____ it a rabbit?
A: _____, _____.

3.

Q: _____ they apples?
A: _____, _____.
　　They are oranges.

13

Super Speaking in Grammar

A. Listen to the conversation and practice with a partner. Use the cues given. Then change roles and practice again. Track 9

Tiffany / a dentist / ?
No ⇨ a painter

Is **Tiffany a dentist?**

No, she isn't **a dentist.** She is **a painter.**

Peter / a teacher / ?
No ⇨ a photographer

the students / from Italy / ?
No ⇨ from Korea

Kim Yuna / a tennis player / ?
No ⇨ a figure skater

B. Work with a partner. You choose a job from the pictures and write it on a piece of paper. Your partner asks questions to find out what he/she is.

teacher

porter

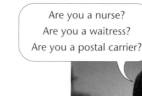

Are you a nurse?
Are you a waitress?
Are you a postal carrier?

No, I'm not.
No, I'm not.
Yes, I am.

painter

photographer

Your turn to ask!

waitress / waiter

mail / postal carrier

nurse

doctor

police officer

cook

singer

athlete

Family

Read and Listen · Track 10

Hi! I'm Abigail and this is my family. These are my parents. This is my younger brother.

Brian _____

Lisa _____

James _____

Abigail _____

* How many people are there in this picture?
* What do they look like?
* Do they look alike?

* How many people are there in your family?
* Do you have any brothers or sisters?

A. Look at the picture above. Complete the blanks 1-6 below with the words from the box.

| mother | husband | sister | daughter | father | son | wife | brother |

1. Lisa – Brian = _mother_ – _son_

2. James – Abigail = _____ – _____

3. James – Lisa = _____ – _____

4. Abigail – Brian = _____ – _____

5. Brian – James = _____ – _____

6. Lisa – Abigail = _____ – _____

B. Listen and write the correct ages next to the names in the picture above. · Track 11

| 11 | 42 | 39 | 6 |

15

Reading Track 12

Families around the World

Hi, my name is Olivia. I live in Canada. I have three brothers and two sisters. I live with my father and mother and two uncles and three aunts. My grandfather and grandmother live with us, too.

Hello. My name is Chan. Now let me tell you about my family. I live in Singapore with my father and mother. My parents are coffee farmers. Most families here are small. I have one brother and one sister. Their names are Li and Mei. My grandfather lives with us, too.

Pleased to meet you! My name is Mina. I live in Korea. I live with my mother and father. I have one brother. He looks like my father. My mother has straight black hair and has black eyes. I look just like my mother. But I act more like my father. We are both left-handed.

A. Fill in the table. Add your family information.

	Olivia	Chan	Mina	Your family
parents	2	2		
brother				
sister				
uncle				
aunt				
grandmother				
grandfather				

my grandfather

my grandmother

The farmer works in the field.

A. Write the correct word for each picture.

family	left-handed	sisters	black eyes	grandfather	uncle

1. _____

2. _____

3. _____

4. _____

5. _____

6. _____

B. Complete Alice's family tree with the words in the box. Then, listen and check your answers.

Track 13

cousin
younger brother
mother
uncle
grandmother
aunt

Bob
grandfather

Olivia
_____

Gordon
father

Lisa
_____

Robert
_____

Joyce
_____

Michael
uncle

Alice

Brian
_____

Elizabeth
_____

John
cousin

17

Dialog · Track 14

Two students:
- Listen to this dialog and fill in the blanks.
- Listen again and check your answers.
- Read it together.

Minji	Is this your mother?
Peter	Yes, that's my mother.
Minji	Wow! You look just _____. You both have a beautiful smile.
Peter	We are also _____.
	Do you _____ your mother or father?
Minji	I look like my father.
Peter	Oh, what does he do?
Minji	He is a _____ and my mother is a _____.
Peter	Wow! And what about your brother?
Minji	He's a wildlife _____.
Peter	What an interesting family! What does your brother look like?
Minji	He has _____ and brown eyes.

Let's Talk Ask and answer the questions about the dialog with your partner.

1. Does Peter look like his father?
   → No, he doesn't. He looks like _____.

2. Is Peter's mother right-handed?
   → No, she isn't. She is _____.

3. What does Minji's brother do?
   → He is _____.

Super Discussion!  ● Track 15

● Discuss the questions below with your classmates.

1. What does your father do?
   ▶ Does your mother work?

2. Describe your family members and their physical appearance.
   ▶ Who's the tallest/shortest in your family?

3. Do you look more like your father or your mother?
   ▶ Tell everyone about them.

4. What does your family do on Sundays?
   ▶ Tell everyone about it.
   ▶ Where do you usually go?

5. Do you live with your grandparents?
   ▶ If not, do you often visit your grandparents?
   ▶ Where do they live?

6. People often say family members look alike and act alike. Do you agree or disagree?
   ▶ Support your opinions.

7. These days 55 percent of households are nuclear families, mostly with one child.
   What do you think of the nuclear family?
   ▶ Support your opinions.

Super Talk!

● Say and write the sentences in the same way.

Sample Sentences	My Sentences
Hello, I'm Jessica and I'm ten years old. There are four people in my family. I have a father, a mother, and an older brother. My brother is a middle school student. My father is a doctor and my mother is a homemaker. On the weekend, my family often has a picnic at a park.	Hello, I'm _____ and I'm _____. There are _____. I have _____. My brother/sister _____. My father is _____. On the weekend, my family _____ _____.

Super Speaking!

A. Listen to the conversation and practice with a partner. Use the cues given. Then change roles and practice again. ⦿ Track 16

four / father / mother / younger sister
➪ my father

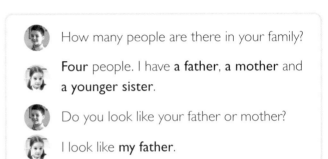

How many people are there in your family?

Four people. I have **a father**, **a mother** and **a younger sister**.

Do you look like your father or mother?

I look like **my father**.

three / father / mother
➪ my mother

four / father / mother / older brother
➪ my father

five / father / mother / two younger sisters
➪ my mother

B. Work in pairs. In turn, ask questions to find out about each other's family and complete the table below.

A: What's your father's name?

_____'s family

	Name(s)	Age	Appearance
Father			
Mother			
Brother(s)			
Sister(s)			

B: ...

A: How old is he?

B: ...

A: What does he look like?

B: He's ... and he has ... hair and ... eyes.

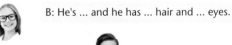

Learn & Practice

- We use *my*, *your*, *his*, *her*, *our*, *their*, *its* to show that something **belongs to someone**. They come in front of nouns.

- **Possessive nouns** *(Tom's / Mary's...)* show belonging. We use an **apostrophe** (') + *-s* to a singular noun or an irregular plural noun. We use only an **apostrophe(')** to a plural noun ending in *-s*.

That is **my** teacher.
His name is William.

I have a sister.
My sister is married.

Ava's dog is a poodle.

The store sells **women's** shoes.

Pronouns	Possessive Adjectives
I	my
you (singular)	your
he	his
she	her
it	its
we	our
you (plural)	your
they	their

A. Look and complete the sentences.

1.

I'm a figure skater.
These are ___my___ iceskates.

2.

Mark is an icehockey player.
That is _____ hockey stick.

3.

Sunny and Kate are students.
That is _____ car.

B. Complete the sentences using the possessive form.

1. _____Rabbits'_____ (Rabbits) ears are long.

2. Those are the _____ (boys) skateboards.

3. _____ (Jane) phone is very expensive.

4. Are these _____ (women) necklaces?

5. _____ (My friend) bicycle is new.

6. That is _____ (Peter) school.

Super Speaking in Grammar

A. Listen to the conversation and practice with a partner. Use the cues given. Then change roles and practice again. ⦿ Track 17

❶

wallet / ?
⇨ Justin / brown

> Is this your **wallet**?
>
> No, it isn't mine.
>
> Whose is it, then?
>
> I think it's **Justin's**. His wallet is **brown**.

❷

hamburger / ?
⇨ Olivia / very big

❸

digital camera / ?
⇨ the children / white

car / ?
⇨ Sally / very old

B. Work with a partner. Ask and answer, as in the example.

nurses   handbags

 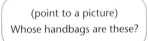

dentist   tools

> (point to a picture)
> Whose handbags are these?

> They're the nurses' handbags.
> Now my turn to ask.

cooks   mixer   taxi driver   taxi

fishermen   nets   children   laptop computer   teacher   dictionaries

Travel

Getting Ready

Read and listen. Work in groups. Practice this conversation. Put a check (√) next to the cities that you have visited. ⊙ Track 18

Ava: Hey Jessica, can you come to my house tonight?

Jessica: Sorry, I can't. I'm packing my suitcase tonight. I'm going to go on a trip around Asia with my parents.

Ava: Around Asia? That's great. Where are you going to start your trip from?

Jessica: We're going to arrive in Seoul on Saturday afternoon. That's our first stop.

- Have you ever traveled abroad?
- Do you like traveling by airplane?
- Which foreign cities would you like to visit? Why?

A. Match the country, city and landmark for each picture. Draw lines from the Country to the City to its Landmark, and write the picture number on the blank.

Country	City	Landmark	Picture Number
Korea	Paris	the N Seoul Tower	4
England	Sydney	the Statue of Liberty	
USA	Seoul	the Eiffel Tower	
China	Rome	the Colosseum	
Italy	Giza	London Bridge	
Australia	Beijing	the Pyramids	
Egypt	New York	the Great Wall	
France	London	the Sydney Opera House	

Where Would You Like to Go?

The beautiful island of Phuket is famous for its fantastic beaches, delicious food, and friendly people. Every year it attracts millions of tourists. It's the perfect place for a week's break. You can relax and sunbathe all day long on one of the island's wonderful beaches. You can also go scuba diving. Many tourists rent a motorbike and travel around the whole island. Patong Beach is the most popular beach among tourists. It is a center of tourism in Phuket. It has white sand, a blue sky, and a blue sea. In the evening you can eat fresh fish in one of Phuket's excellent restaurants, then enjoy a quiet walk along the beach under the stars. Visiting Phuket is the dream of many tourists throughout the world.

island

delicious pizza

tourists

sunbathe

scuba diving

popular actress

A. Write the correct word for each picture.

sand   suitcase   motorbike   beach   sea   world

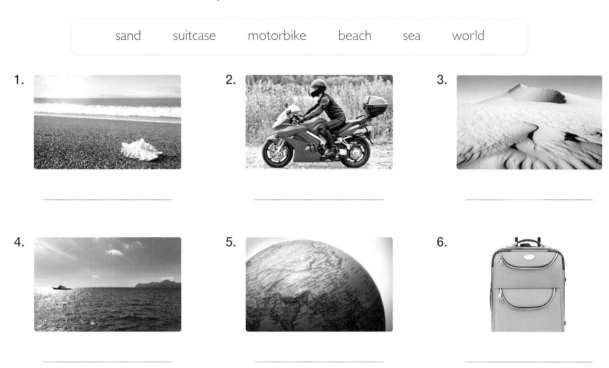

1. _____

2. _____

3. _____

4. _____

5. _____

6. _____

Super Activity!

A. These pictures show some part of an airport. Listen and check (✓) the correct pictures. 🔘 Track 20

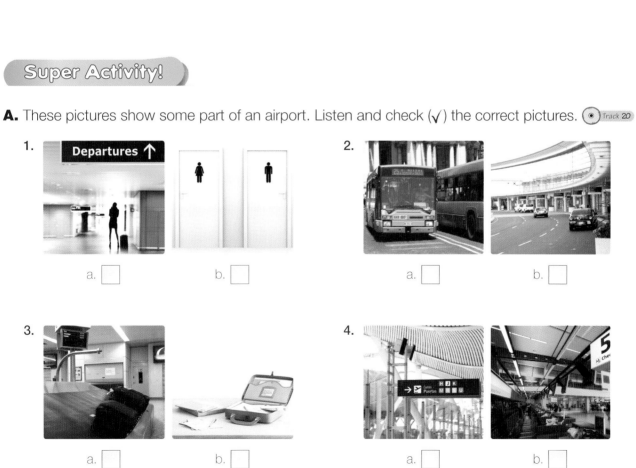

1.   a. ☐   b. ☐

2.   a. ☐   b. ☐

3.   a. ☐   b. ☐

4.   a. ☐   b. ☐

Dialog Track 21

Two students:

- Listen to this dialog and fill in the blanks.
- Listen again and check your answers.
- Read it together (change roles).

Travel Agent	Hi! How can I help you?
Tom	I'd like to book a _____ to Jeju island.
Travel Agent	Yes, good choice. Jeju island is _____ beautiful this time of year. _____ do you want to book for?
Tom	Two – myself and my new wife. It's for our honeymoon.
Travel Agent	Congratulations! You couldn't have picked a more romantic _____. When are you looking to go?
Tom	From July 21st until August 6th.
Travel Agent	_____ a hotel from this brochure?
Tom	Okay. Ah, what about this one?

 Track 22

Brazil is the largest country in South America and it is the fifth largest country in the world. Its population is about 200 million and the official language is Portuguese.

The Amazon

It is one of the longest rivers in the world and it flows from west to east across South America. It's about 6,800 km long and it doesn't have any bridges!

The Capital City

Brasilia is one of the most modern cities in the world. It's got lots of interesting buildings.

The Carnival City

Its name means 'River of January', but there's no river in Rio! It's famous for its beaches and, of course, the carnival, as they call it!

Track 23

● Discuss the questions below with your classmates.

1. Have you ever traveled abroad?

   Yes! Where have you been? Tell everyone about it.

   No! Where would you like to go?

2. How many countries have you traveled to?

   ▶ What did you do and see in those countries?

3. What country/city would you like to travel to next?

   ▶ When are you going to go?

   ▶ Who are you going to go with?

   ▶ How long are you going to go for?

   ▶ What are you going to do there?

   ▶ What kinds of things do you think you will buy?

4. Describe the most interesting person you met on one of your travels.

5. Do you like to travel with parents?

   Yes! Why?   **No!** Why not?

6. What is your favorite method of travel at your destination?

   ▶ Train? Bus? Boat? Bicycle? Backpacking?

7. What was the most interesting place you have ever visited?

   ▶ What is the most interesting city to visit in your country?

Super Talk!

● Say and write the sentences in the same way.

Sample Sentences

   I'm on vacation in Seoul this week. My hotel is very nice and comfortable. The people are very friendly. The food is delicious and cheap. The restaurants are wonderful! Seoul is beautiful. It is a big city with lots of new buildings. To visit Seoul is the dream of tourists.

My Sentences

   I'm on vacation in _____. My hotel is _____ and _____. The people _____. The food _____. The restaurants _____. _____ is beautiful. It is a big city with _____ _____. To visit _____ _____.

Super Speaking!

A. Listen to the conversation and practice with a partner. Use the cues given. Then change roles and practice again. ⊙ Track 24

Korea / ?
Yes ⇨ Seoul
some museum exhibits

Have you been to **Korea**?

Yes, I went to **Seoul** last summer.

What did you do?

I saw **some museum exhibits**.

❷
England / ?
Yes ⇨ London
Buckingham Palace

❸
France / ?
Yes ⇨ Paris
the Eiffel Tower

❹
the United States / ?
Yes ⇨ Los Angeles
Disneyland

B. Listen and repeat the dialog. Then use the speaking cards to practice it with your partner.

⊙ Track 25

A: Where did you go on vacation this summer?

B: I went ❶ _____ to Hawaii _____ .

A: Who did you go with?

B: I went with my ❷ _____ family _____ .

A: What else did you do together?

B: We ❸ _____ swam every day _____ . It was so much fun!

A: Did you meet any new people there?

B: Yeah, the people were really ❹ _____ friendly _____ .

❶ to Seoul
❷ friends
❸ visited the N
   Seoul Tower
❹ kind

❶ to Sydney
❷ cousin
❸ went to
   beaches
❹ nice

Language Focus!

Learn & Practice

- We use *be going to* + base verb to make **predictions about the future** (when we have evidence for that at present time).

- We use *be going to* + base verb to talk about our **plans for the future** (when we intend to do in the future).

It **is going to** rain soon.

We**'re going to** go to Switzerland in December.

- To make negative forms, we put *not* after *be* verb.

- In a Yes/No question, put *am*, *are*, or *is* before the subject.

They're **not** going to watch TV tonight.
They're going to play tennis.

Q: **Is** she **going to** sell her car?
A: **Yes**, she **is**. / **No**, she **isn't**.

A. Read and complete the sentences as in the example.

1. I _am going to play_ (play) basketball.

2. You _____ (go) shopping.

3. He _____ (study) Korean.

4. She _____ (walk) the puppy.

5. We _____ (clean) the house.

6. They _____ (buy) some books.

B. Look at the pictures and answer the questions.

1.

by train

Q: Are they going to travel by airplane?

A: _No, they aren't. They're_ _going to travel by train_

2.

a new cell phone

Q: Is Kevin going to buy a new bicycle?

A: _____

_____ .

3.

a horse

Q: Are you going to ride a bicycle?

A: _____

_____ .

29

Super Speaking in Grammar

A. Listen to the conversation and practice with a partner. Use the cues given. Then change roles and practice again. ⊙ Track 26

tomorrow / ?
⇨ go shopping

 What are you going to do **tomorrow**?

I'm going to **go shopping**.

tomorrow morning / ?
⇨ take the dog for a walk

tomorrow night / ?
⇨ watch a scary movie

this weekend / ?
⇨ visit my grandparents

tomorrow afternoon / ?
⇨ get a haircut

at 9:00 tomorrow morning / ?
⇨ write an email

this summer / ?
⇨ travel to Europe

B. Work with a partner. Look at the Parker family's schedule for next week. Ask and answer questions using the prompts as in the example.

Is Olivia going to play computer games on Sunday?

No, she isn't. She's going to play badminton with her father.

Your turn to ask!

Sunday:	Olivia – play badminton with her father
Monday:	Mrs. Parker – water the plants
Tuesday:	Peter – meet his friends
Wednesday:	Mr. Parker – repair the car
Thursday:	Peter – play tennis with his mother
Saturday:	Olivia and Peter – watch a DVD

1. Mrs. Parker / water the plants / on Monday / ?
2. Peter / study math / on Tuesday / ?
3. Mr. Parker / make a cake / on Wednesday / ?
4. Peter / study in a library / on Thursday / ?
5. Olivia and Peter / visit their aunt / on Saturday / ?

Unit 4

In My Free Time

Track 27

Ann: What do you do in your free time?

Ken: I usually play computer games. What about you?

Ann: I usually enjoy reading comic books in my free time. Time really flies when I read them.

What do you do in your free time? ❋ What do you usually do in the evening?

A. Look at the pictures below. Then match the correct phrases to each picture.

☐ ☐ ☐ ☐

☐ ☐ ☐ ☐

a. play a musical instrument	b. jump rope	c. do taekwondo	d. do yoga
e. listen to music	f. surf the Internet	g. play soccer	h. watch TV/a DVD

31

Reading Track 28

How Do You Spend Your Free Time?

Sarah

I prefer indoor activities. When I have some free time, I like reading, watching TV, going to the movie theater, or listening to music. My favorite hobby, however, is collecting things. I have a great soccer card collection. I have ten cards from Brazil, five cards from Japan, and fifteen cards from Spain. I trade cards with my friends after school.

I like indoor and outdoor activities. Soccer is a really interesting game. I play on my school team. It's fun. Sometimes I go to watch international games with my dad. He's a big fan, too. I have an autographed soccer ball from the Korean team.

Peter

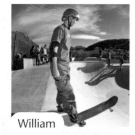

William

I love outdoor activities. I enjoy cycling, skiing, and surfing, but my favorite hobby is definitely skateboarding. It's exciting, and it's fun. I'd like to be a professional skateboarder, so I always practice about two to three hours after school. I also practice during the weekend, of course.

movie theater

soccer ball

autograph

cycling

surfing

skateboarding

A. Match the phrases with the pictures 1-8.

1.
2.
3.
4.
5.
6.
7.
8.

surf the Internet _____

read a book _____

enjoy surfing _____

do yoga _____

go to the movies _____

do taekwondo _____

play soccer _____

watch the international game _____

A. People are talking about entertainment. Listen and number the correct pictures. (●) Track 29

1.
   ☐

2.
   ☐

3.
   ☐

4.
   ☐

Dialog Track 30

Two students:

- Listen to this dialog and fill in the blanks.
- Listen again and check your answers.
- Read it together (change roles).

Betty	_____ in your free time?
Eric	Well, I usually play soccer for my school.
Betty	_____ do you play?
Eric	We play once a week, on _____.
Betty	Do you play other sports?
Eric	Yes, I do. I _____ with my older brother.
Betty	Does he go to your school?
Eric	No, he doesn't. He goes to university. _____?
Betty	No, I don't.
Eric	What do you do in your free time?
Betty	I usually play the guitar.
Eric	That's cool! I'd love to learn _____ someday.
Betty	I'd be happy to teach you.
Eric	Really? Thanks!

Answer the Questions

1. Does Eric usually play the guitar in his free time?

2. Does Betty like playing basketball?

3. How often does Eric play soccer?

● Discuss the questions below with your classmates.

1. What do you usually do in your free time?

   ▶ Tell everyone about your free time.

2. Do you like to watch movies/DVDs?

   Yes! ⤳ What kind of movie do you like?

   What is your favorite movie?

   No! ⤳ Why not?

3. Who do you spend your free time with?

4. Do you have a favorite hobby?

   Yes! ⤳ What is it? Tell everyone about it.

   No! ⤳ Why not?

5. What is your favorite sport?

   ▶ What is it? Tell everyone about it.

6. Where do young people in your country usually spend their free time?

7. Do men and women spend their free time differently?

   ▶ How?

8. Are there any activities that you used to do but don't do anymore?

   ▶ Why did you stop?

Super Talk!

● Say and write the sentences in the same way.

Sample Sentences	My Sentences
Saturday is my favorite day of the week. In the morning I always get up late, at 11:00. I usually have a big breakfast. In the afternoon I always go rock climbing. It's a difficult sport, but I'm very good at it. In the evening I'm usually very tired, but I always go out with my friends. We often go to the movies. We're all horror film fans.	_____ is my favorite day of the week. In the morning I _____ _____. In the afternoon I _____ _____. In the evening _____ _____ _____.

35

Super Speaking!

A. Listen to the conversation and practice with a partner. Use the cues given. Then change roles and practice again. 🔘 Track 32

do yoga / ?
⇨ twice a week

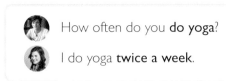

How often do you **do yoga**?

I do yoga **twice a week**.

go to the movies / ?
⇨ once a month

play soccer / ?
⇨ every morning

do taekwondo / ?
⇨ five times a week

B. Listen and repeat the dialog. Then use the speaking cards to practice it with your partner.

🔘 Track 33

A: What do you do in your free time, Kevin?

B: I usually ❶ _____ read a book _____ or ❷ _____ watch TV _____.
What about you?

A: I usually ❸ _____ do yoga _____.
But sometimes I ❹ _____ go swimming _____.

B: That's great!

❶ listen to music
❷ play badminton
❸ do aerobics
❹ go out with friends

❶ ride my bicycle
❷ play the guitar
❸ surf the Internet
❹ go camping

Learn & Practice

- *Do/Does* is placed **before the subject** to make a **Yes/No question** in simple present.

Q: **Does** she wear glasses?
A: **No**, she **doesn't**.
Q: **Does** she read a book in her free time?
A: **Yes**, she **does**.

Yes/No Questions			
Do	I/you/we/they	play	sports?
Does	he/she	go	to university?
Does	it	finish	late?

- We use *how often* to ask about the **frequency of an action**. We use **frequency adverbs** to talk about how often we do something. They usually go **before** the **main verb**, but **after** the **verb be**.

always	-	usually	-	often	-	sometimes	-	seldom	-	rarely	-	never
(100%)		(about 90%)	(about 70%)			(about 50%)		(about 10%)		(about 5%)		(0%)

- The question word *what* asks about **information**. (What + do/does + subject + base verb ...?)

Q: **How often** does Kelly go shopping?
A: She goes shopping **once a week**.

Q: **What** do you do in your free time?
A: I **usually** listen to K-pop music.

A. Circle the correct words and match them to their answers.

1. (Do / Does) they walk to school?   a. No, she doesn't.

2. (Do / Does) Bob like basketball?   b. Yes, they do.

3. (Do / Does) she read a newspaper?   c. No, he doesn't.

B. Rewrite the sentences with the given words.

1. I take a shower. (sometimes)   ⇨   _____

2. She jogs in the morning. (always)   ⇨   _____

3. He is late for school. (often)   ⇨   _____

In My Free Time

Super Speaking in Grammar

A. Listen to the conversation and practice with a partner. Use the cues given. Then change roles and practice again. (◉) Track 34

❶

Michelle / play the piano / ?
⇨ play the guitar

> Does **Michelle play the piano**?
>
> No, she doesn't.
>
> What does she **play**?
>
> She **plays the guitar**.

❷

Sunny / make cakes / ?
⇨ make cookies

❸

Kevin and Lucy / enjoy skiing / ?
⇨ enjoy snowboardingmake

❹

Brian / like pizza / ?
⇨ like cheeseburgers

B. Work with a partner. Look at the table. Taking turns, ask and answer questions as in the example.

	play computer games	see friends	take out the trash
Sarah	never	always	once a week
Joseph and Ashley	sometimes	usually	twice a week
Raymond	usually	sometimes	three times a week

How often does Sarah watch TV?

She never watches TV.

How often does Sarah take out the trash?

She takes out the trash once a week.

take out the trash

Food

First read about Sarah and match the correct words to each picture. Then listen and check your answers. ⊙ Track 35

a. vegetables   b. toast
c. meat   d. apple
e. bacon cheeseburgers
f. pizza   g. orange juice
h. green tea

My food and drink!
I have breakfast at seven-thirty. I have cereal with milk, [ ] and jam, and some [ ].
I have lunch at the cafeteria at one o'clock.
I eat some [ ] and an [ ] or an orange. I finish lunch with some [ ].
In my family, we have dinner at seven o'clock. We eat a lot of different things, for example [ ] or [ ] with [ ]. There's also chocolate cake for dessert.

❈ What time do you have breakfast?   ❈ What do you eat and drink for breakfast?
❈ Where do you have lunch/dinner?   ❈ What's your favorite food and drink?

39

Reading ⦿ Track 36

STREET FOOD

Sandwiches, hot dogs, and doughnuts are popular all over the world. But many countries have their own special kinds of street food, too.

Fish and chips is popular street food in the UK. People buy it in special shops and eat it out of a paper bag.

Crepes are a French speciality. They came from the Brittany region of northwestern France. There are various different types of crepes. There are sweet crepes with chocolate or jam. But crepes with cheese, tomato and mushrooms are also delicious! They are popular in many other countries around the world as well.

Mexican tacos are a traditional Mexican dish. They are thin corn pancakes with meat, beans, cheese, and tomato sauce. They are quick to cook and easy to buy because they are very cheap. They're really spicy!

Ramen is a popular Korean noodle dish. It is a cheap and tasty meal. It is also popular in Japan because it is a symbol of long life.

doughnuts

paper bag

mushroom

beans

spicy

noodles

A. Draw a circle around the right words and then write the words.

1.

Do you want _____ for breakfast?
(sandwiches / hamburgers)

2.

He saved a lot of money to _____ a new car.
(eat / buy)

3.

People eat fruit in _____ ways.
(various / popular)

4.

Snow, steam, and ice are _____ forms of water.
(different / same)

5.

Kimchi is a Korean _____ food.
(traditional / cheap)

6.

The woman is ordering a _____ at a restaurant.
(note / meal)

Super Activity!

A. Listen and match each person with their breakfast. (⊙) Track 37

1.

Sally ☐

2.

Greg ☐

3.

Amy ☐

B. Listen and check (✓) the correct answer to the questions. (⊙) Track 38

1. a. I'll be ready to go in 30 minutes. _____
   b. Yes, I'd like to have a salad first. _____

2. a. I can't stand meat. _____
   b. I like fish better. _____

3. a. I'll eat it here. _____
   b. I don't usually eat hamburgers. _____

Dialog Track 39

Two students:

- Listen to this dialog and fill in the blanks.
- Listen again and check your answers.
- Read it together (change roles).

Waiter	Good evening. What can I get you?
Customer	Um, I'm not _____ yet.
	Can I have a minute or two?
Waiter	Certainly. Take your time.
	(*A few minutes later.*)
Waiter	Can I take your order now?
Customer	Yes, I think so. I'd like _____ to start with.
Waiter	And for the main course?
Customer	I'd like a burger.
Waiter	_____ burger would you like?
Customer	What do you recommend, the double cheeseburger or the bacon cheeseburger?
Waiter	Both are good, but I prefer the bacon cheeseburger.
Customer	Okay, I'd like the bacon cheeseburger.
Waiter	_____?
Customer	I'd like _____ mineral water, please.
Waiter	Thank you.

Answer the Questions

Check (√) T for true or F for false.

	T	F
1. The customer is in a seafood restaurant.	☐	☐
2. The waiter dislikes the bacon cheeseburger.	☐	☐
3. The customer wants the double cheeseburger.	☐	☐
4. The customer wants a bottle of mineral water.	☐	☐

● Discuss the questions below with your classmates.

1. What is your favorite food?
　▶ Why do you like it?
　▶ Tell everyone about it.

2. Do you like Korean food?
　Yes! ▷ Why?　　No! ▷ Why not?
　▶ What kind of Korean food do you like best?

3. Can you cook?
　▶ What can you make?

4. What do you have for breakfast?

5. Do you have a big meal for lunch or for dinner?
　Yes! ▷ Why?　　No! ▷ Why not?

6. Do you eat a lot of fruit and vegetables?
　Yes! ▷ Why?　　No! ▷ Why not?
　▶ Do you know any healthy foods? Tell everyone about healthy eating.

7. At what times do you usually eat your meals?
　▶ Breakfast?　　▶ Lunch?　　▶ Dinner?

8. Do you like food from other countries?
　▶ If yes, which do you like the most?

Super Talk!

● Say and write the sentences in the same way.

Sample Sentences

　Do you eat healthy food for breakfast, lunch, and dinner? It's important. Apples, watermelons, and grapes are healthy, but too much ice cream is unhealthy. I love carrots and potatoes. They are healthy, but French fries are not healthy.

My Sentences

　Do you eat healthy food for breakfast, lunch, and dinner? It's important. _____, _____, and _____ are healthy, but too much _____. I love/like _____ _____. They are healthy, but _____ _____ not healthy.

Super Speaking!

A. Listen to the conversation and practice with a partner. Use the cues given. Then change roles and practice again. ⊙ Track 41

❶

a Coke
⇨ the double cheeseburger

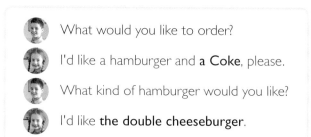

What would you like to order?

I'd like a hamburger and **a Coke**, please.

What kind of hamburger would you like?

I'd like **the double cheeseburger**.

❷

a bottle of water
⇨ the chicken burger

❸

a Coke
⇨ the shrimp burger

❹

a glass of orange juice
⇨ the bacon cheeseburger

B. Work with a partner. Fill in the table about you. Then ask your partner the questions and complete the table about him/her.

What kind of food do you like?

Well, I like salad, but I don't like broccoli.

	Your Partner	You
1. What kind of food do you like?		
2. Which foods don't you like?		
3. What time do you have breakfast?		
4. How often do you eat at a fast food restaurant?		
5. What's your favorite fast food meal?		
6. What's your favorite fast food restaurant?		
7. What do you usually have for dinner?		

Learn & Practice

- We use **a** when a word begins with a consonant sound: *b, c, d, f, k, l, t, w, y*, etc.
  We use **an** when the word begins with the vowels *a, e, i, o* and *u*. We use **a/an** in front of **singular countable nouns**. Remember that *a* and *an* mean **one**.
- We use **some** to say the amount when we don't know how much.
- We use **some** for both countable and uncountable nouns.

It is **a** dog.

It is **an** elephant.

There is **an** apple. There are **some** biscuits, and there's **some** milk.

	Countable Nouns	Uncountable Nouns
a/an	a fork an orange	water milk
some	some forks some apples	some water some milk

A. Write *a, an* or *some*.

1. __an__ ant
2. _____ juice
3. _____ octopus
4. _____ camera
5. _____ leaves
6. _____ bottle

B. Look and write *a, an* or *some*.

1.

I have __some__ money.

2.

There is _____ guitar.

3.

She has _____ milk.

4.

I see _____ airplane.

5.

It is _____ car.

6.

We want _____ eggs.

45

Super Speaking in Grammar

A. Listen to the conversation and practice with a partner. Use the cues given. Then change roles and practice again.

your father
⇨ engineer

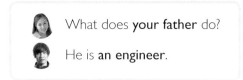

What does **your father** do?

He is **an engineer**.

your brother
⇨ firefighter

your mother
⇨ architect

your uncle
⇨ taxi driver

Kathy
⇨ teacher

B. Work with a partner. Look at the picture. Taking turns, ask and answer questions as in the example.

1. water / on the table / ?
   No ⇨ orange juice

2. doughnuts / on the table / ?
   No ⇨ bread

3. lemons / on the table / ?
   No ⇨ strawberries

4. pencils / on the table / ?
   No ⇨ cups

5. knives / on the table / ?
   No ⇨ forks

Is there any water on the table?

No, there isn't any water. There is some orange juice.

Your turn to ask!

Unit 6 *Shopping*

Getting Ready

Read and listen to the conversation. Match it to picture a, b, or c.  Track 43

Shop assistant:	Can I help you?
Customer:	Yes, I'm looking for a dress.
Shop assistant:	What size are you?
Customer:	It's for my daughter.
Shop assistant:	What size is she?
Customer:	I think she's medium.
Shop assistant:	What color?
Customer:	Pink.
Shop assistant:	Do you like this one?
Customer:	How much is it?
Shop assistant:	It's seven dollars.

What is the woman buying in picture A?

Where do you buy your clothes?

Do you like shopping for clothes?

Do you like shopping with friends or alone?

Shopping and Prices

shop assistant
money
customer

S (small)   M (medium)

L (large)   XL (extra large)

PRICES

£257 Two hundred and fifty-seven pounds

$284 Two hundred and eighty-four dollars

€290 Two hundred and ninety euros

£3.50 Three pounds fifty

$5.60 Five dollars and sixty cents

€5.90 Five euros and ninety cents

A. Listen and repeat the prices. ⏺ Track 44

$4.50   £39   €10.99   £75.42 $25

B. Match the pictures with the words.

swimsuit ☐   sneakers ☐

T-shirt ☐   boots ☐

sun hat ☐   bag ☐

jeans ☐   socks ☐

①  $24
② $7
③ $5
④ $2

⑤ $10
⑥ $30
⑦ $15
⑧ $9

Pair Work Practice the conversation below. Then ask and answer questions about other things with your partner using the words above.

A: Can I help you?

B: How much is this ❶____T-shirt____?

(How much are these ❷____socks____?)

A: It's ❸__seven dollars__. (They are ❹__two dollars__ a pair.)

B: Thanks.

A: You're welcome.

A. Customers are talking to salespeople in a store. Do the customers make a purchase? Listen and check (✓) *Yes* or *No*. ◉ Track 45

	Yes	No
1.	☐	☐
2.	☐	☐
3.	☐	☐

B. Look and answer the questions.

American Money

dollar: $1, one dollar/a dollar bill

dollar: $5, five-dollar bill

penny: 1 ¢
    one cent
    a penny

nickel: 5 ¢
    five cents
    a nickel

quarter: 25 ¢
    twenty-five cents
    a quarter

dime: 10 ¢
    ten cents
    a dime

1. How much is two dimes and a nickel? ⇨ _____25 cents_____

2. How much is three quarters? ⇨ _____

3. How much is five pennies? ⇨ _____

4. How much is five cents and four nickels? ⇨ _____

5. How much is ten dimes? ⇨ _____

Dialog ⊙ Track 46

Two students:

● Listen to this dialog and fill in the blanks.
● Listen again and check your answers.
● Read it together (change roles).

Shop assistant	_____ with anything?
Customer	Yes, I'd like a leather jacket, please.
	_____ any black jackets?
Shop assistant	Of course. This jacket is very popular.
	It does _____ on you.
Customer	Yes, but don't you think it's _____?
Shop assistant	What size are you?
Customer	Do you have it in _____?
Shop assistant	Here you are.
Customer	It's cool! _____?
Shop assistant	It's on sale. Let's see... It's $99.
Customer	It's _____ for me.
Shop assistant	But it's a nice jacket, sir.
Customer	You're right. _____. Here's $100.
Shop assistant	Thank you very much and here's your change.
Customer	Thanks.

Answer the Questions

Check (√) T for true or F for false.

		T	F
1.	The customer is in a bookstore.	☐	☐
2.	The customer wants to buy a leather jacket.	☐	☐
3.	The assistant thinks that the black jacket is too big.	☐	☐
4.	The man wants to pay by credit card.	☐	☐

Super Discussion!

Track 47

Discuss the questions below with your classmates.

1. Do you like going shopping?

> **Yes!** → Why? Tell everyone your opinions.
>
> **No!** → Why not? Tell everyone your opinions.

2. Would you be happy to buy something over the Internet?

3. What kinds of items do you like to go shopping for?

> ▶ Why do you like them?

4. Which do you prefer: saving money or spending money?

5. What's the most expensive thing you've ever bought?

> ▶ Do you shop around for the cheapest price?

6. Which is better, shopping in shops or shopping online?

> ▶ Tell everyone your opinions.

7. Do you like going shopping in other countries?

> **Yes!** Why? Tell everyone your opinions.
>
> **No!** Why not? Tell everyone your opinions.

8. Is window shopping a total waste of time?

> ▶ What is 'window shopping'? Do you like to window-shop?

Match the shops in the box to the correct pictures.

| a butcher's | _e_ | a hairdresser's | _____ | a bakery | _____ | a clothes shop | _____ |
| a post office | _____ | a gift shop | _____ | a dry-cleaner's | _____ | a pharmacy | _____ |

Super Speaking!

A. Listen to the conversation and practice with a partner. Use the cues given. Then change roles and practice again. ⊙ Track 48

❶

shirt / ?
⇨ $45

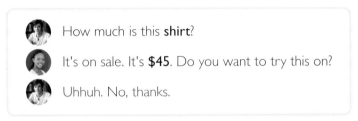

How much is this **shirt**?

It's on sale. It's **$45**. Do you want to try this on?

Uhhuh. No, thanks.

❷

short-sleeved shirt / ?
⇨ $35

❸

sweater / ?
⇨ $38

❹

blouse / ?
⇨ $47

B. Listen and repeat the dialog. Then use the speaking cards to practice it with your partner.

⊙ Track 49

A: Excuse me, I'm looking for some ❶ __bracelets__ .
It's for my ❷ __wife's__ birthday.
B: I'd like to recommend this one.
It looks really good on every ❸ __lady__ .
A: What's the price?
B: It's ❹ __90 dollars__ . But it's on sale now.
You can get 10% off.

❶ earrings
❷ daughter's
❸ girl
❹ 50 dollars

❶ jeans
❷ son's
❸ boy
❹ 60 dollars

Learn & Practice

- We use the **Present Progressive** to talk about things you are doing right now. We form the **Present Progressive** with the present of the verb *be* and the base **verb + -*ing***.

That girl **is looking** at me!
She **is drinking** water.

Subject	*Be* Verb	Verb + -*ing*
I	am	reading. working. smiling. singing.
He, She, It...	is	
You, We, They	are	

- We use the pronoun *one* in the **singular** and *ones* in the **plural** so that we do not repeat the noun.

A: Do you like the red tie?
B: No, I like this **one** (tie).

I never wear red shoes.
I always wear black **ones** (shoes).

A. Complete the sentences with the *Present Progressive* of the verbs in brackets.

1.
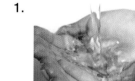
wash

He ____is washing____ his hands.

2.

wait

The students _____ for a bus.

3.

listen

She _____ to music.

B. Complete the sentences with *one* or *ones*.

1. A: Which is your phone?

B: The white ___one___ .

2. A: Can I borrow your dictionary?

B: Sorry, I haven't got _____ .

3. A: Which pants fit you better?

B: The black _____ .

4. A: I need a ticket.

B: I have _____ .

Super Speaking in Grammar

A. Listen to the conversation and practice with a partner. Use the cues given. Then change roles and practice again. Track 50

Sarah
⇨ play the flute

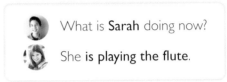

What is **Sarah** doing now?

She **is playing the flute**.

Kimberly
⇨ talk on the phone

they
⇨ watch TV

Philip
⇨ eat an apple

B. Which of the items below did you buy? Work with a partner. Ask questions and answer them as in the example.

red shoes   green shoes

I'd like to look at some shoes.

Which ones do you want to buy?

I want to buy the red ones.

Your turn now!

purple dress   black dress

green socks   pink socks

gray sweatshirt

blue sweatshirt

blue skirt

brown skirt

white T-shirt

green T-shirt

Unit 7 — Everyday Activities

Read and listen to the conversation. Work in pairs. Practice the conversation. ⊙ Track 51

What are you doing?

I'm doing my homework.

No, I'm not. I'm making dinner.

Are you doing the laundry?

※ Did you have breakfast today?

※ What time do you usually have breakfast?

※ How many hours do you watch TV every week?

※ Which activity do you usually do for fun?

◎ Which activities can you see in the pictures? Tell the class.

- doing homework
- doing the house work
- making dinner
- talking on the phone
- having a snack
- playing the violin
- watching TV
- washing the dishes
- doing the laundry
- listening to a CD
- having dinner
- reading a book

55

Reading Track 52

A Day in My Life

Nancy is a student. She gets up at 6:30 every morning. It's early, but she always feeds the animals before she has breakfast. She leaves home at 8:00 and goes to school by bicycle. She gets home at about 4:00. She usually helps her father on the farm. Then, she rides her horse, Punch. After dinner, she sometimes washes the dishes. She watches a DVD for an hour, but she never stays up late. She goes to bed at ten o'clock.

Judy is a student. She usually gets up about seven o'clock. She always takes a shower before she has breakfast. Her school isn't far, so she walks with her friends. She has lunch at school at twelve o'clock. Her father has a pet shop. After school, she often helps him. She usually

takes care of the animals. Then, she sometimes goes to the movie theater with some friends. After dinner, she plays computer games or calls her friends and talks on the phone for hours. She goes to bed at about 11:30.

● Who's the country girl? Who's the city girl?

A. Match the times to the clocks.

1. six twenty   •
2. five thirty-five •
3. eleven thirty   •
4. three o'clock   •
5. seven oh-five   •
6. four forty-five   •

• 11:30
• 07:05
• 05:35
• 04:45
• 03:00
• 06:20

feed

animals

take a shower

take care of

A. Match the sentences and the pictures. Complete with *He's, She's,* or *They're.*

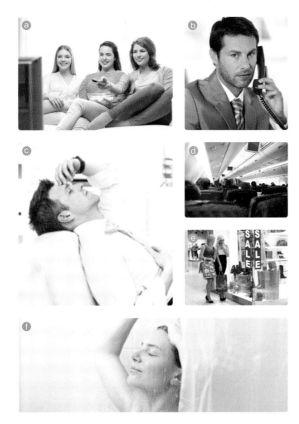

1. ___She's___ having a shower. [f]

2. _____ sleeping. [ ]

3. _____ talking on the phone. [ ]

4. _____ watching TV. [ ]

5. _____ sitting on a plane. [ ]

6. _____ shopping. [ ]

B. Listen and check (√) the correct answer. ⊙ Track 53

1.

   a. He is watching TV.

   b. He is talking on the phone.

   c. He is reading a book.

2.

   a. She is waiting for a bus.

   b. She is standing next to a bench.

   c. She is waiting at the airport.

3.

   a. They are studying in the library.

   b. They are having lunch at the cafeteria.

   c. They are playing soccer.

Track 54

Two students:
- Listen to this dialog and fill in the blanks.
- Listen again and check your answers.
- Read it together (change roles).

Mother	Jennifer, you've got homework and then _____.
Jennifer	Oh, Mom. It's not. This is my _____.
Mother	But it is _____.
Jennifer	Mom, I always go to bed at _____,
	and I read in bed until _____.
Mother	You go to bed at _____ on the weekend.
	You go to bed at nine o'clock on school days.
Jennifer	But Mom...
Mother	That's enough, Jennifer. You've got school tomorrow. Good night!
Jennifer	But Mom, I _____ tomorrow. Tomorrow is Saturday!

Listen and Repeat Track 55

What time is it?

| It's two o'clock. | It's two-oh-five. | It's two twenty-five. | It's two thirty. | It's two forty-five. | It's two fifty. |

Pair Work Practice the conversation with your partner using the clocks above.

A: What time is it, please?

B: _____*It's two o'clock.*_____

A: Thank you.

● Discuss the questions below with your classmates.

1. What time do you usually wake up?

2. What do you do in the afternoons?
 ▷ Tell everyone about it.

3. What do you do in the evenings?
 ▷ What time do you go to bed?
 ▷ Tell everyone about it.

4. What time do you go to school?
 ▷ What do you do between classes?

5. Do you have a favorite activity?
 Yes! What is it? Tell everyone about it.
 No! Why not?

6. Describe a typical daily routine.
 ▷ Tell everyone about your daily routine.

Super Talk!

● Say and write the sentences in the same way.

Sample Sentences

My sister and I are busy every day. She gets up at six o'clock in the morning. I get up at seven o'clock. We have breakfast at the same time. My sister goes to school at eight o'clock and I go to school at nine o'clock. We do our homework in the afternoon. Then she rides her bicycle and I read a book. We have dinner at eight o'clock and go to bed at nine thirty.

My Sentences

_____ and I are busy every day. _____
_____ in the morning. I _____.
We _____
goes to school _____ and I _____.
We _____.
Then _____.
We have dinner _____.

Super Speaking!

A. Listen to the conversation and practice with a partner. Use the cues given. Then change roles and practice again. ( ) Track 57

Betty / do her homework / ?
⇨ listen to K-pop music

Is Betty doing her homework?

No, she isn't.

What is she doing now?

She **is listening to K-pop music.**

Abigail / watch TV / ?
⇨ clean the house

they / learn yoga / ?
⇨ eat lunch

Julia / talk on the phone / ?
⇨ read a book

B. Work with a partner. Talk about when you normally do these activities.

get up	go to bed	go to work/school	finish work/school	have dinner

When do you usually get up?

I usually get up at seven o'clock.

When do you go to the movies?

I go to the movies on Friday afternoon.

see friends
go to the movies
watch TV
play sports
have an English class
go shopping

on

Monday	morning
Tuesday	
Wednesday	
Thursday	afternoon
Friday	
Saturday	
Sunday	evening

60

Learn & **Practice**

- To form the **negative** of the Present Progressive, we use *not* after the verb *be* and the verb + *-ing*. To make a yes/no question, we put *am*, *are*, or *is* before the subject.

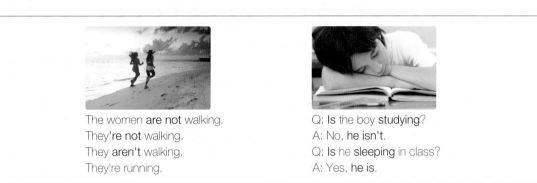

The women **are not** walking.
They**'re not** walking.
They **aren't** walking.
They're running.

Q: **Is** the boy **studying**?
A: No, he **isn't**.
Q: **Is** he **sleeping** in class?
A: Yes, he **is**.

- We use *when* and *what time* for questions about **time**. We use *at* for times of the day and for the expression *at* night.

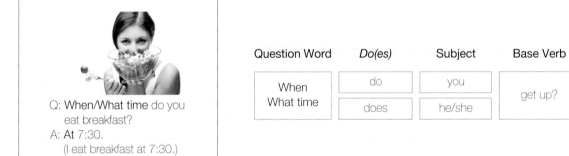

Q: When/What time do you eat breakfast?
A: At 7:30.
(I eat breakfast at 7:30.)

Question Word	Do(es)	Subject	Base Verb
When What time	do	you	get up?
	does	he/she	

A. Make questions and answers.

1. The man is crying.

   Q: Is the man crying?

   A: Yes, he is.   No, he isn't.

2. She is sitting on the chair.

   Q: _____

   A: _____   _____

3. Kevin and Lisa are learning yoga.

   Q: _____

   A: _____   _____

Super Speaking in Grammar

A. Listen to the conversation and practice with a partner. Use the cues given. Then change roles and practice again. Track 58

they / run / ?
No ⇨ walk

Are they running?

No, they aren't. They **are walking**.

the girl / have dinner / ?
No ⇨ read a book

Peter / watch TV / ?
No ⇨ study Korean

Ava and Karen / eat pizza / ?
No ⇨ walk to school

B. Work with a partner. Taking turns, ask and answer questions using *when* or *what time*.

When/What time
do you eat breakfast?

I usually eat breakfast
at eight o'clock.

1. wake up

2. usually get up

3. eat/have breakfast

4. leave home in the morning

5. usually get to class

6. eat/have lunch

7. get home from school

8. eat/have dinner

9. usually study in the evening

10. go to bed

Unit 8

Health

Read and listen to the conversation. Work in pairs. Practice the conversation. ⦿ Track 59

What's wrong with you?

I've got a stomachache.

You should go to the doctor.

Have you ever been sick?

How often do you get a cold?

⧉ What do you usually do when you don't feel well?

⧉ When did you last go to the doctor's? What for?

A. Look at the picture. How does each person feel? Match them to the health problems (1-8).

1. toothache: _____Tim_____
2. a broken arm: _____
3. a sore throat: _____
4. a cold/(the) flu: _____
5. a fever: _____
6. a headache: _____
7. (a) stomachache: _____
8. measles: _____

63

Healthy Food

In Korea, doctors are worried because teenagers eat a lot of junk food. Most teenagers don't eat enough fruit or vegetables. Many young people are overweight. They often eat unhealthy food and spend a lot of time sitting in front of the television or the computer. Some teenagers say that they don't have time to eat healthy food, but children who have a poor diet often have health problems when they are older. Eating a healthy, well-balanced diet can help you feel better and live longer.

Here's some advice:

- Have some vegetables or some fruit in every meal. Tomatoes and green vegetables are great!
- Eat five small meals a day instead of two or three large meals.
- It's a good idea to eat snacks, but don't eat a lot of sugar. Have some bread, an apple, some grapes, or a carrot.
- Don't eat fried food very often. Have some rice or some pasta instead.
- Drink a lot of water. If you want a sweet drink, have some fruit juice.
- Do some exercise every day. Exercise burns off the calories and makes you fit.
- Finally, remember – there's no need to be skinny! Enjoy your food and have fun when you're exercising.

A. Write the correct word for each picture.

| fast food | unhealthy | fried food | vegetables | healthy | overweight |

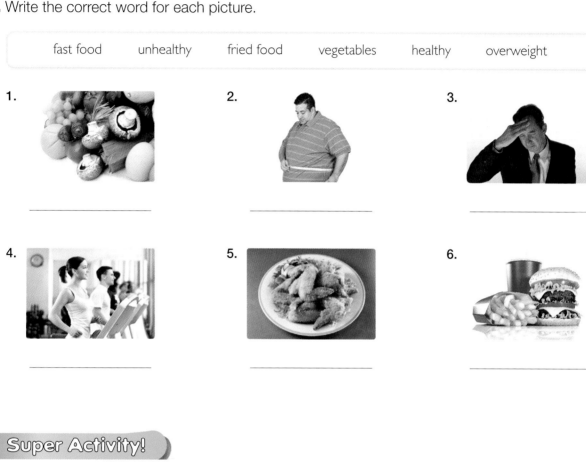

1.

2.

3.

4. _____

5. _____

6. _____

Super Activity!

A. Listen and match the numbers with the correct pictures. Track 61

1.
☐

2.
☐

3.
☐

4.
☐

B. Listen and check (√) the most suitable answer. Track 62

1. a. _____ Yes, I go jogging every day.
   b. _____ No, I don't drink coffee.

2. a. _____ Wow! You look so healthy.
   b. _____ Take this medicine every night.

3. a. _____ I feel funny. I have a bad headache. I think I have a fever, too.
   b. _____ I go jogging every day and go hiking on the weekend.

Dialog Track 63

Two students:

- Listen to this dialog and fill in the blanks.
- Listen again and check your answers.
- Read it together (change roles).

Eric	Hi, Sara. Where were you last Saturday? You _____ to the library.
Sara	Hi! I really wanted to, but I couldn't.
Eric	Why? What was the matter with you?
Sara	I had _____ on Friday night and I _____ all night.
Eric	Did you take a _____?
Sara	Yes, I did. But it didn't work, so I had to go to the dentist's. My tooth was decayed and he had to _____.
Eric	Poor you! Did it hurt?
Sara	Of course, it did. I could only drink some water. I couldn't speak for some time.
Eric	Oh, no! _____?
Sara	I am fine, thanks. I should go now. See you tomorrow.
Eric	See you.

Answer the Questions

Check (√) T for true or F for false.

	T	F
1. Sara couldn't go to the library because of an earache.	☐	☐
2. Sara took a painkiller.	☐	☐
3. The dentist examined her tooth and decided to pull it out.	☐	☐
4. After the dentist pulled her tooth out, she could eat something.	☐	☐
5. Sara is fine now.	☐	☐

● Track 64

● Discuss the questions below with your classmates.

1. How often do you get a cold?
  ▸ How long were you sick?

2. Have you ever had an operation or a broken bone?
  ▸ Tell everybody about your experience.

3. What do you do to exercise and stay fit?
  ▸ How often do you exercise?
  ▸ Why do you like it?

4. How does food/exercise/the weather affect our health?
  ▸ Explain your opinion.

5. Does anyone in your family smoke?
  ▸ Do you think smoking is not bad for your health?

6. What do you do to stay healthy?
  ▸ Tell everyone about it.

7. What is healthy food?
  ▸ Do you pay much attention to what you eat?
  ▸ Do you think it is more important for you to eat healthy or tasty food?

8. Did you ever miss school because you were sick?

9. Do you have any allergies?

10. Do you eat a lot of healthy food? What do you eat?

Super Speaking!

A. Listen to the conversation and practice with a partner. Use the cues given. Then change roles and practice again. Track 65

❶

Sharon / a fever and a cough
⇨ take some medicine

 What's the matter with **Sharon**? She doesn't look well.

 She has **a fever and a cough**.

 She should **take some medicine**.

❷

Nicole / a sore arm
⇨ not play tennis

❸

Walter / a toothache
⇨ go to the dentist

❹

Megan / a headache
⇨ lie down and rest

B. Listen and repeat the dialog. Then use the speaking cards to practice it with your partner.

Track 66

A: Hello, ❶ ___Diana___ . Are you OK?

B: No, I feel terrible.

A: Oh, dear. What's wrong with you?

B: I have ❷ ___a sore throat___ .
  I should ❸ ___have ice cream___ .

A: I think you shouldn't have ice cream.
  You should ❹ ___have a hot drink___ .

❶ Sunny
❷ a cold
❸ take a shower
❹ take a break

❶ Nancy
❷ a stomachache
❸ eat that hamburger
❹ lie down and rest

Learn & Practice

- We use *should* to give advice. *Should* means it's a **good idea to do something**.

- We use *shouldn't (= should not)* when it's a **bad idea to do something**.

Susan has a cold.

She **should** see a doctor.

She **shouldn't** eat ice cream.

- We use the verb *have (got)* and *has (got)* to show that **something belongs to somebody**.

- We use the verb *have (got)* and *has (got)* to describe people, animals, or things.

He **has got** the flu.

He **has got** a fever, too.

He **has got** a thermometer in his mouth.

He **has got** an ice pack on her head.

He **has got** a rag doll.

	Have			*Has*	
I/We			He		
You	have got a daughter.		She	has got a problem.	
They			It		

* We usually use **have got** and **has got** in conversations or in letters and emails to friends. **Have got** has the same meaning as *have*.

* In short answers, Q: Have you got a pen? A: Yes, I have. (O) / Yes, I. (X)

A. Complete the sentences. Use *should* or *shouldn't*.

1.

do

You ___*should do*___ your homework.

2.

not / be

They _____ late for school.

3.

take

You _____ some medicine.

4.

not / watch

You _____ TV so much.

Super Speaking in Grammar

A. Listen to the conversation and practice with a partner. Use the cues given. Then change roles and practice again. (Track 67)

① Brian / a camcorder / ?
No ⇨ He's / a digital camera

> Has **Brian** got a **camcorder**?
> No, he hasn't. **He's** got **a digital camera**.

② Betty / short hair / ?
No ⇨ She's / long hair

③ Lauren / a black and white cat / ?
No ⇨ She's / a black cat

④ they / notebooks / ?
No ⇨ They've / cups

B. Work with a partner. Taking turns, give advice. Use *You should...* followed by the phrases in the box.

get an alarm clock	go to the post office	wash them	study harder
put some sunscreen on	get a new one	hurry	see a doctor
cut it	renew them		

1. I didn't pass my exam.
2. I'm not feeling well.
3. My flight leaves in one hour.
4. My clothes are dirty.
5. I need to send this package to Korea.
6. My hair is too long.
7. My television doesn't work anymore.
8. I'm going to lie in the sun this morning.
9. My books are due at the library, but I still need them.
10. I overslept and was late for work again.

I didn't pass my exam.

You should study harder.

School Life

Read and listen to the conversation. Work in pairs. Practice the conversation. Track 68

Cindy: What's your favorite subject?

Ken: My favorite subject is Korean history. What's yours?

Cindy: I love English. I like my English teacher.

Ken: I see. Did you get a good grade in the last test?

Cindy: Sure. I got an A.

Ken: Wow! Can you help me with my English?

Cindy: Why not? Let's study together.

Ken: Thank you.

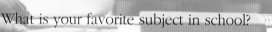

What is your favorite subject in school?

What is your least favorite subject?

Why do you like that subject?

Why don't you like it?

A. Look at the pictures below. Then match the school subjects in the box with the pictures.

a. physical education (P.E.)   b. English   c. geography   d. music

e. math   f. science   g. history   h. art

At School

Hello, my blog friends! I'm Suji Lee from Seoul, Korea. I'm going to tell you about my school day. The school starts at 9 a.m. Each class is for 50 minutes with a 10 minute break. We all study twelve subjects. My favorite subject is English. I like my English teacher. He has a lot of classes at our school, but he's never tired. He's always helpful, patient, and funny. I like lunchtime. After the 4th class in the morning, I have lunch with my friends in the cafeteria. I like *bulgogi*, but I don't

like fast food. After lunch, I surf the web or read a book. School is over at 3:30 p.m. After school, we must clean our classroom. My favorite day is Friday because the next day is Saturday and I don't have to go to school. How about your school life?

Hi. I'm Eric from Sydney, Australia. My school is a little different from yours. Every day my morning classes begin at 8:30 in the morning. We have six classes a day. We go to different rooms for different classes. We all study five core subjects and choose three more. My favorite subject is geography. I'm interested in Korean history, too. We don't have a break between classes. Instead, we have morning tea time from 10:10 to 10:40 a.m. I usually drink milk and eat cookies. At lunchtime, I eat fast food, usually a hamburger and French fries. School ends at 3:15 p.m. After school, I play volleyball with my team members for about an hour. Then I go home and help my parents around the house. I'm usually very tired by the end of the week. On the weekend, I don't have to get up early because I don't have classes.

A. Write the correct word under each picture. Use the words from the box.

lunchtime

geography

school

different

volleyball

tired

1.

_____

2.

_____

3.

_____

4.

_____

5.

_____

6.

_____

Super Activity!

A. Listen and choose the subjects each girl likes. ⊙ Track 70

1. a.

b.

2. a.

b.

B. Listen and check (✓) what students are talking about. ⊙ Track 71

1. _____   a. science exam

   _____   b. math exam

2. _____   a. being late for school

   _____   b. being absent from school

Dialog Track 72

Two students:
● Listen to this dialog and fill in the blanks.
● Listen again and check your answers.
● Read it together (change roles).

Sharon	What are the _____, Alex?
Alex	Well, we _____ school uniforms. We can't listen to music in the classrooms or hallways. But we can listen to it in the music room.
Sharon	Uh-huh.
Alex	And we _____ in the classrooms, but we can eat in the lunchroom.
Sharon	Oh. And can I bring my _____ to school?
Alex	Yes, you can. But you can't use your phone in class.
Sharon	Do we _____ clean up after class?
Alex	Yes, we have. Everyone _____ clean up every day. What else? Oh, you can't fight with anyone. That makes the teachers _____.

Answer the Questions

Check (√) T for true or F for false.

	T	F
1. They don't have to wear school uniforms.	☐	☐
2. They can listen to music in the music room.	☐	☐
3. They mustn't bring their cell phones to school.	☐	☐
4. They have to clean up every day.	☐	☐

● Discuss the questions below with your classmates.

1. What are your teachers like?

▷ Describe the teacher you like most.

▷ Describe the teacher you like least.

2. Does your English teacher come from Canada?

Yes! Do you like your English teacher?

No! Where does he/she come from? Do you like your English teacher?

3. How many students are there in your class?

▷ How many students do you think there should be in a class?

4. What do you prefer a male teacher or a female teacher?

▷ Explain the reasons.

5. Do you like your school rules?

No! Why not? Please explain.

6. What subjects do you study in school? List them here.

_____   _____   _____

_____   _____   _____

_____   _____   _____

_____   _____   _____

7. Are you always on time for school?

Yes! How do you do it?

No! Why not? Please explain.

8. Do you like to study English?

Yes! Why do you study English?

No! Why not? Share your reasons.

9. Have you ever been late for class?

▷ If so, why?

▷ When was the last time?

▷ Did your teacher get angry?

Super Speaking!

A. Listen to the conversation and practice with a partner. Use the cues given. Then change roles and practice again. ⊙ Track 74

P.E. ⇨ fun

 What's your favorite subject?

 My favorite subject is **P.E.**

 Why do you like **P.E.**?

 Because it's **fun**.

science ⇨ interesting

math ⇨ exciting

music ⇨ relaxing

B. Listen and repeat the dialog. Then use the speaking cards to practice it with your partner.

 Track 75

A: Hi, ❶___Jane___. How are you doing?

B: Pretty good. What about you?

A: I'm tired. The ❷___English homework___ is too difficult.

B: I can help you. We can do it together after school.

A: Thank you, Jane. Are you interested in ❸___math___?

B: Yes, it's my favorite subject.

A: Why do you like it?

B: I like ❹___to solve the math questions___.

❶ Tom
❷ math homework
❸ English
❹ my English teacher

❶ Ava
❷ science homework
❸ history
❹ to learn about the events of the past

Learn & Practice

- We use *can* to give **permission**. To make a sentence negative, we add *not* after *can*.
- We also use *Can I...?* to ask for **permission**.

You **can't** go out alone at night.

Can I have a look at that red shirt?

- We use *must* for **rules or strong advice**. When we use *must*, we have no choice. We use *must not* (= *mustn't*) to say that something is **against the rules or the law**.

You **must** wear your seatbelt.

You **mustn't** park here.

A. Look at the signs and write what you *must* or *mustn't* do.

1.

swim in this river

⇨ You mustn't swim in this river.

2.

stop

⇨ _____

3.

use your phone

⇨ _____

4.

turn left

⇨ _____

B. Make questions with *Can I...?*

1. You're speaking to your brother. You want a glass of water.

⇨ (have)   Can I have a glass of water?

2. You're speaking to your sister. You're going to turn on the TV.

⇨ (turn on) _____

Super Speaking in Grammar

A. Listen to the conversation and practice with a partner. Use the cues given. Then change roles and practice again. Track 76

①

Can I **wear jeans**?

No, you can't. We must **wear school uniforms**.

wear jeans / ?
No ⇨ wear school uniforms

② bring my MP3 player / ?
No ⇨ listen to music in music class

③ bring my lunch box / ?
No ⇨ eat school food

④ arrive late for school / ?
No ⇨ arrive at school before 8:00 a.m.

B. Work with a partner. Make sentences about your school rules. Use *must* or *mustn't* with the given phrases.

We must listen to the teacher in class.

We mustn't draw on the wall.

Your turn now!

1. listen to the teacher in class
2. draw on the wall
3. do our homework
4. bring our cell phones to school
5. clean up after class
6. eat school food
7. wear school uniforms
8. be quiet in class
9. arrive late for class
10. fight with anyone
11. run in the hallway
12. use our personal computers

Special Days

Getting Ready

**Read and listen to the conversation. Work in pairs.
Practice the conversation.** Track 77

Jim: When's your birthday, Jennifer?
Jennifer: My birthday's on May fifteenth. When is your birthday?
Jim: My birthday is on September sixth. What do you usually do on your birthday?
Jennifer: I usually meet my friends and have a birthday party.

When's your birthday?   ✽ Which day do you like best in a year? Why?

A. Listen and repeat. Track 78

1st first	2nd second	3rd third	4th fourth	5th fifth
6th sixth	7th seventh	8th eighth	9th ninth	10th tenth
11th eleventh	12th twelfth	13th thirteenth	14th fourteenth	15th fifteenth
16th sixteenth	17th seventeenth	18th eighteenth	19th nineteenth	20th twentieth
21st twenty-first	22nd twenty-second	23rd twenty-third	24th twenty-fourth	25th twenty-fifth
26th twenty-sixth	27th twenty-seventh	28th twenty-eighth	29th twenty-ninth	30th thirtieth
31st thirty-first				

B. Listen and repeat the months of the year.

Track 79

1. January
2. February
3. March
4. April
5. May
6. June
7. July
8. August
9. September
10. October
11. November
12. December

C. Listen and match the names and the birthdays. Track 80

1. Sunny   2. Tom   3. Jason

May 15th   August 5th   April 3rd

Reading Track 81

Doljabi Event

Doljanchi is a traditional Korean custom for the first birthday of a child. The first birthday has a special meaning in Korean culture, and some people believe that the first birthday is an opportunity to pray for blessings for the child's future. The highlight for the party is *doljabi. Dol* means first birthday. *Jabi* means "picking up" or "grabbing". Parents put various items on a special table. The baby has to pick up an object from the table. They believe that the item the baby chooses determines his or her future. Guests try to predict what the baby will choose.

Parents put a bow and arrow, a rice cake, and yarn on the table. They wish their child to be a general, eat well, and live long. Sometimes, a book, a pencil, and money are also put on the table. This means that they want him or her to be a scholar and rich, too. If the child chooses a stethoscope, it is expected that he or she will be a medical doctor.

Foreigners often wonder why Korean people celebrate the 1st birthday party and throw such an extravagant party. One reason is that, in the past, the death rates for children were high and many children died before their first birthday, so a baby's first birthday was very important to the baby and his or her parents.

 Track 82

Mother's Day

People celebrate Mother's Day all around the world. Each year on this special day children show their mothers how much they love them.

Thanksgiving

In the USA, people celebrate Thanksgiving on the fourth Thursday in November. They give thanks for the things they've got.

Building Vocabulary

A. Write the correct word under each picture. Use the words from the box.

a bow and arrow

stethoscope

general

birthday

parents

yarn

1.

birthday

2.

_____

3.

_____

4.

_____

5.

_____

6.

_____

Super Activity!

A. Listen and check (✓) the date. Track 83

1. a. October 14th _____
   b. October 4th _____

2. a. April 13th _____
   b. April 3rd _____

3. a. July 21st _____
   b. July 31st _____

4. a. February 5th _____
   b. February 15th _____

B. Listen and write T for true, F for false.  Track 84

1. Kathy's favorite day is Valentine's Day. _____

2. William goes to the beach with his friends. _____

3. Independence Day is on the 4th of July. _____

Dialog Track 85

Two students:
- Listen to this dialog and fill in the blanks.
- Listen again and check your answers.
- Read it together (change roles).

Mina	When is Halloween?
Peter	I think it's _____ on October 31st.
Mina	What do you know about Halloween?
Peter	On Halloween, young children _____ as ghosts and monsters. In the early evening, they go from door to door _____ candy. When you open the door, the children shout, "Trick or Treat!" Then you hand out _____ to each child's bag.
	Later, the children go to Halloween parties or get together to tell scary stories. Some people believe that ghosts and monsters _____ on Halloween. So children _____ as ghosts or monsters to receive the real ghosts and monsters.
	What do you do on New Year's Day in Korea?
Mina	We go to my grandma's house. We greet our elders with a full bow. Then, they give us New Year's greeting money.
Peter	That's _____.

 Track 86

 **In Canada,** friends and family put butter on child's nose for good luck.

In Nepal, people make a special mark on the child's forehead. The mark is made from a mixture of rice, yoghurt, and coloring. They think that the mark will bring good luck on their birthday.

In Argentina, girls have a big birthday party on their 15th birthday. At the party, the birthday girl dances with her father and friends.

In Denmark, people put a flag  outside their window to show that somebody in the house is having a birthday. The family put presents around the child's bed at night. When the child wakes up, he or she sees them in the morning.

82

Super Discussion! ⊙ Track 87

● Discuss the questions below with your classmates.

1. When is your birthday?
   ➤ What activities do you usually do on your birthday?
   ➤ What is the best birthday gift you have ever received?

2. Does your family celebrate Christmas? When is Christmas?
   Yes!   Describe a typical Christmas Day in your household.
   No!   Why not?

3. Did you get any presents on Valentine's Day?
   ➤ Did you give anyone gifts on Valentine's Day?
   ➤ When is Valentine's Day?

4. What special food do people usually eat for Christmas, Thanksgiving, New Year's or Birthday?

5. Think about a public holiday in Korea.
   ➤ Why do you think that it is important?
   ➤ What do people usually do that day?
   ➤ Tell everyone about that day.

6. What special days/holidays (for example: Parents' Day, Teacher's Day, Children's Day) do you celebrate in your country?
   ➤ How do you celebrate these special days?

7. What do you usually do on New Year's Eve?
   ➤ What do people usually do that day?
   ➤ Tell everyone about that day.

8. How is Halloween celebrated in your country?
   ➤ Do you believe in ghosts?
   ➤ What makes you afraid of ghosts?

Super Speaking!

A. Listen to the conversation and practice with a partner. Use the cues given. Then change roles and practice again. Track 88

Kevin / ?
November 11th
meet my friends and have a birthday party

 When's your birthday, **Kevin**?

 My birthday is on **November 11th**.

 What do you usually do on your birthday?

 I **meet my friends and have a birthday party**.

Ashley / ?
December 14th
go to a restaurant with my family

Edward / ?
August 19th
watch a magic show with my family

Joseph / ?
October 22nd
go to the movies with my family

B. Listen and repeat the dialog. Then use the speaking cards to practice it with your partner.

 Track 89

A: What is your favorite ❶ _____Korean holiday_____?

B: My favorite Korean holiday is ❷ ___New Year's Day___.

A: Why do you like it?

B: Because I ❸ ___received money from my parents and relatives___.

A: When is it?

B: It is ❹ _____on the first day of January_____.

❶ American holiday
❷ Christmas
❸ can get a lot of presents
❹ on December twenty-fifth

❶ Korean holiday
❷ Chuseok
❸ love visiting my grandparents who live on Jeju Island
❹ on August fifteenth on the Lunar Calendar

Prepositions of Time / Infinitive of Purpose

Learn & Practice

- We use *on* with **days** and **dates**. We use *in* for parts of the **day** and with **months, seasons**, and **years** (**e.g.** *in the morning, in July, in the summer, in 1999*).

I got married **on** December 31st.

days:	on Monday
	on New Year's Day
	on Christmas Day
dates:	on May 6th
part of a particular day:	on Friday morning
	on Saturday night
adjective + day:	on a cold day

- We use an **infinitive** to talk about the **reason** or **purpose** for doing something (why someone does something). In more formal English, we use *in order to*.

Q: Why did she go to the zoo?
A: She went to the zoo **to see** animals.

She went to the zoo **in order to see** animals. (Formal)

A. Write *in* or *on*.

1. _____ the winter
2. _____ Tuesday morning
3. _____ 2002
4. _____ May 10th
5. _____ Thursday
6. _____ the evening

B. Complete the sentences. Choose from the box.

> to see who it was   to buy some books   to watch the news
> to learn Korean   to study economics

1. I turned on the television *to watch the news* _____ .

2. I'd like to go to Seoul _____ .

3. The doorbell rang, so I looked out the window _____ .

4. Anthony wants to go to college _____ .

5. She went to the bookstore _____ .

Super Speaking in Grammar

A. Listen to the conversation and practice with a partner. Use the cues given. Then change roles and practice again. ⊙ Track 90

When do you **go snowboarding**?

I go snowboarding on **Saturday afternoon**.

when / go snowboarding / ?
⇨ Saturday afternoon

when / have English class / ?
⇨ Tuesday mornings

when / go on vacation / ?
⇨ the first day of August

when / celebrate Christmas / ?
⇨ December 25th

B. Work with a partner. Taking turns, ask and answer questions as in the example.

Lauren went to florist's.
Reason: order some flowers

Why did Lauren go to florist's?

She went to florist's to order some flowers.

Your turn to ask!

Diana went to the coffee shop.
Reason: meet her friend

Janet went to the library.
Reason: borrow some books

Walter went to the theater.
Reason: see *The Phantom of the Opera*

Jessica went to the airport.
Reason: see off her friends

Richard and Alice went to Paris.
Reason: see the Eiffel Tower

The children recycled old newspapers and books.
Reason: protect the environment

Unit 11

My Dream Job

Read and listen to the conversation. Work in pairs. Practice the conversation. ⊙ Track 91

What does your sister do?

That's my sister.

She's a journalist.

What do you want to be?

I want to be a teacher.

⚜ What jobs do you know?

⚜ What do you want to be in the future? Why?

A. Match the jobs with the pictures.

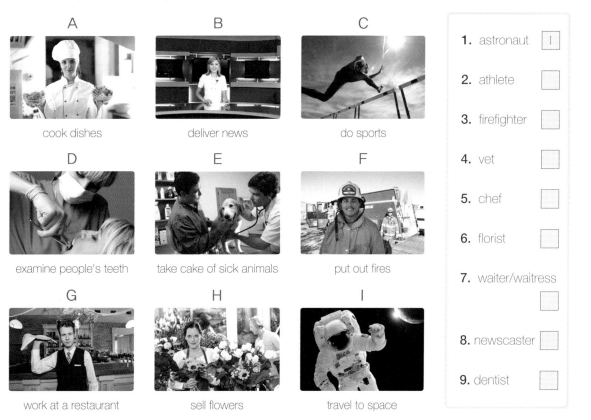

A	B	C
cook dishes	deliver news	do sports
D	E	F
examine people's teeth	take cake of sick animals	put out fires
G	H	I
work at a restaurant	sell flowers	travel to space

1. astronaut ☐ I
2. athlete ☐
3. firefighter ☐
4. vet ☐
5. chef ☐
6. florist ☐
7. waiter/waitress ☐
8. newscaster ☐
9. dentist ☐

87

Reading Track 92

When I Grow Up

Hi, I'm Tiffany. There are lots of amazing jobs in the world. It is hard to choose just one. When I grow up, I want to be a flight attendant. I want to travel all over the world and learn to speak different languages. It would be exciting to meet new people every day. I think this would be a good job for me because I'm a very active and responsible person. To be a flight attendant, I should try to be friends with many people. I should study more to improve my English, too. I think being a flight attendant would be a very exciting job and would make me feel happy.

Hi, I'm Ava. I'd like to do something exciting! I'd like to be an astronaut! I don't want to be famous, but I want an interesting job. I'd like to travel to space and discover incredible things. It would be exciting to walk on the moon and bring back some space rock! I'd like to live in space for a few weeks and find out what it's really like. Someday I'll be the first woman on Mars!

language

flight attendant

rock

88

A. Draw a circle around the correct words and then write the words.

1.

He quits his _____ all at once.
(job / travel)

2.

At this time of night, I _____ so alone.
(fall / feel)

3.

She is _____ as a singer.
(famous / exciting)

4.

We _____ new facts by using science.
(travel / discover)

Super Activity!

A. Listen and number the pictures. Then listen again, and circle the words used to describe each job. Track 93

☐

fun

boring

☐

dangerous

stressful

☐

tird

interesting

B. Listen and follow the directions. Track 94

1. What are Kathy and Harry talking about?

a. part-time job   b. job interview   c. full-time job

2. Who is Harry?

a.   b.   c.

Dialog ◉ Track 95

Two students:

● Listen to this dialog and fill in the blanks.
● Listen again and check your answers.
● Read it together (change roles).

Sam   What do you do _____?

Maria   I'm an English teacher.

Sam   Do you like teaching children?

Maria   Oh, yes! I love working with kids.

         They're so _____.

Sam   That must be nice. What are your hours like?

Maria   I _____ Monday to Friday, _____ eight

         _____ five.

Sam   Well, I guess you have the _____!

Maria   Yeah, I like it a lot. There's just one thing I _____.

Sam   What's that?

Maria   The distance to school. It's too _____. It takes me an hour to

         drive there every day.

Sam   Wow. That must be awful!

Maria   It is, but the schools that are near me are not as good. And what about you?

         What do you do?

Sam   I'm a _____. I talk with many _____ every day.

         It's interesting to meet many people, but it _____ be

         _____ if the customer is unhappy!

Answer the Questions

Check (√) T for true or F for false.   T   F

1. Maria is an airline pilot.   ☐   ☐

2. Sam works in a hospital.   ☐   ☐

3. A salesperson's job is never stressful.   ☐   ☐

● Discuss the questions below with your classmates.

1. What do you want to do when you grow up?
  ▷ What kind of job do you want to do?
  ▷ Why do you want to do it?

2. What jobs do you do at home?

3. Are there jobs that are only for women or only for men?
  ▷ Tell everyone about them.

4. Do you think parents should choose jobs for their children?
  Yes! ▷▷ Why?
  No! ▷▷ Why not?

5. What do you think the job of being an English teacher is like?

6. Who has the best job in the world?
  ▷ Why do you think so?

7. What are some common jobs in your country?
  ▷ What are some common jobs for men in your country?
  ▷ What are some common jobs for women in your country?

8. Is being a housewife a job?
  ▷ Should women get paid for this?

9. What is the most interesting part-time job you have had in your life?

Super Speaking!

A. Listen to the conversation and practice with a partner. Use the cues given. Then change roles and practice again. Track 97

father / a chef
⇨ a teacher

What does your **father** do?

He's **a chef**.

What do you want to be?

I want to be **a teacher**.

uncle / an airline pilot
⇨ an actress

mother / a physical therapist
⇨ a tennis player

older sister / a fashion designer
⇨ a computer programmer

B. Listen and repeat the dialog. Then use the speaking cards to practice it with your partner.

Track 98

A: What do you want to be when you grow up?

B: You mean after I finish school?

A: Yeah. What do you want to become?

B: When I was younger, I wanted to become ❶ _____ a lawyer _____ ,
but now I want a job that lets me ❷ _____ travel _____ .

A: Does that mean you want to be ❸ _____ a photographer _____ ?

B: No, I want to be ❹ _____ a flight attendant _____ .

❶ a teacher
❷ travel and meet new people
❸ a flight attendant
❹ an airline pilot

❶ a journalist
❷ help other people
❸ a teacher
❹ a nurse

Learn & Practice

- We use the **simple present** to tell repeated actions and things that are always true. When the subject is the **third person singular**, add *-s* or *-es* to the base form of a verb.

 Jessica eat**s** breakfast every morning.

She walk**s** to school.

She stud**ies** Korean every day.

-s	work ⇨ work**s** eat ⇨ eat**s** open ⇨ open**s** write ⇨ write**s**	• Add *-s* to most verbs if the subject is singular.
-es	watch ⇨ watch**es** wash ⇨ wash**es** fix ⇨ fix**es** go ⇨ go**es** pass ⇨ pass**es**	• Add *-es* to verbs that end with *-ch*, *-sh*, *-x*, *-o*, or *-ss*.
-ies	study ⇨ stud**ies** fly ⇨ fl**ies** cry ⇨ cr**ies**	• If a verb ends in a **consonant** + *-y*, change the *-y* to *-i* and add *-es*.
Irregular	have ⇨ has	• No rules

- We use *want* and *would like* to talk about things we want. The meaning is the same, but *would like* is usually more polite than *want*.

- We use *would like* with a noun or an infinitive (*to* + the base verb). In a questions, we use *would* before the subject.

I'm hungry. I **want** a sandwich.
I'm hungry. I**'d like** a sandwich.

Subject	*Would Like*	Object
I/You/ He/She/ We/They/Tom	would like 'd like wouldn't like	a noun OR an infinitive

A. Change the sentences by using *would like*.

1. He wants a bottle of water.   ⇨ _He would like_ _____ a bottle of water.

2. Do you want a cup of coffee?   ⇨ _____ a cup of coffee?

3. Olivia wants some cheese on her pasta. ⇨ _____ some cheese on her pasta.

4. They want to go snowboarding.   ⇨ _____ snowboarding.

Super Speaking in Grammar

A. Listen to the conversation and practice with a partner. Use the cues given. Then change roles and practice again. (Track 99)

see a movie tomorrow / ?
⇨ do the laundry

> Would you like to **see a movie tomorrow**?
>
> I'd like to, but I can't. I have to **do the laundry**.
>
> That's too bad.

go skating tomorrow / ?
⇨ study math

go to the amusement park tomorrow / ?
⇨ babysit my little sister

go to the beach tomorrow / ?
⇨ clean my room

B. Work with a partner. Read the information about the animals on the table below. Taking turns, ask and answer questions as in the example.

	Elephants	Crocodiles	Brown bears	Hippopotamuses
LIVE	in Africa	in Africa	in North America	in Africa
EAT	leaves, fruit, plants	meat	berries, honey, fish, meat	plants
LIKE	water	the sun	honey	water

> Where do elephants live?
> What do crocodiles eat?
> What do hippopotamuses like?

> They live in Africa.
> They eat meat.
> They like water.

Getting Ready   Read and listen to the conversation. Work in pairs.
Practice the conversation. Track 100

Do you play any sports?

I enjoy playing soccer and basketball.

How often do you play soccer?

I always play soccer. It's my favorite sport.

How often do you exercise?

What's your favorite sport?

What sports do you think are dangerous?

Can you swim?

A. Look at the pictures below. Then match the sports in the box with the pictures.

a. cricket	b. taekwondo	c. volleyball	d. surfing
e. aerobics	f. yoga	g. canoeing	h. gymnastics

95

Reading Track 101

My Extreme Sport!

Hi! My name's Amy. I am a student at the Hudson School in New York. I don't like indoor sports, but I love outdoor sports and activities. On Mondays I play basketball at school with my friends. On Tuesdays we play volleyball, and on Wednesdays we go canoeing. Thursday is my favorite day of the week. In the evening I play cricket. I play for the school team. On Fridays my friends and I don't play any sports. Instead, we go to a party. We don't have to go to school on weekends. On Saturdays I do yoga with my mother. On Sundays I stay at home watching movies with my family. Yesterday I saw a woman surfing on TV and it looked like a lot of fun. I can swim, but I can't surf. I don't know how to surf, so I decided to join our school sports club. I want to learn how to surf. It will be exciting to surf on top of a big wave in the ocean.

A. Work with a partner. Ask and answer these questions.

 1. Is Amy in the school football team?

No, she isn't. She is in the _____.

 2. Why does Amy want to join the school sports club?

She wants to learn _____.

 3. Why does Amy want to learn how to do it?

She saw a woman _____ on TV and it looked like _____.

A. Which of the activities are used with *do*, *go*, or *play*?

volleyball	cricket	yoga	taekwondo
canoeing	aerobics	surfing	basketball

1.

do taekwondo

2.

play volleyball

3.

go canoeing

4.

_____

5.

_____

6.

_____

7.

_____

8.

_____

Super Activity!

A. Listen to the different conversations and write what each person does for fun. Then listen again and write how often they do it. ⊙ Track 102

Name	What?	How often?
1. Ava	judo	three times a week
2. Peter		
3. Ava's father		
4. Michelle		

B. Listen and circle the right answer to the following questions. ⊙ Track 103

1. What does Kevin usually do after work?

   a. go rollerblading   b. work out in the gym

2. Who is Kevin?

   a.    b.    c.

Dialog Track 104

Two students:

● Listen to the dialog and fill in the blanks.
● Listen again and check your answers.
● Read it together (change roles).

Jessica	You're in great shape, Paul.
	Do you _____ at a gym?
Paul	Yeah, I do. I guess I'm a real
	_____.
Jessica	So, _____ do you work out?
Paul	Well, I do aerobics every day after work.
	And then I play racquetball.
	How about you?
	_____ on the
	weekends?
Jessica	No, I hate sports.
Paul	Really? So _____
	on the weekends?
Jessica	Uh, I watch my favorite programs on TV.
	I guess I'm a real couch potato.
Paul	You need _____
	right now. Otherwise, you might be in big
	trouble.

Answer the Questions

Check (√) T for true or F for false.

	T	F
1. Paul works out in a stadium.	☐	☐
2. Jessica is a real fitness freak.	☐	☐
3. Jessica's favorite sport is playing badminton.	☐	☐
4. Paul does aerobics and plays racquetball every day after work.	☐	☐

● Discuss the questions below with your classmates.

1. What's your favorite sport?
- How often do you play it?
- What other sports do you like?

2. Do you ever go to a gym? How often do you go?
- What do you do there?

3. How many hours of sports do you have in school?
- Is this enough?

4. What sports do you watch on TV?
- Who's your favorite athlete? Why?

5. What kinds of sports do you do on the weekend?
- What did you do last weekend?

6. What sports do you think are dangerous?
- What can happen?
- Tell everyone about your opinion.

7. What sports are popular in your country?
- Tell everyone about them.

8. Do you prefer playing or watching sports?
- Why?

9. What do you want to learn if you join an Extreme Sports Club?
- Tell everyone about it.

rock climbing

mountain bike

bungee jumping

hang gliding

motor racing

Super Speaking!

A. Listen to the conversation and practice with a partner. Use the cues given. Then change roles and practice again. ⊙ Track **106**

tennis
⇨ swimming

What's your favorite sport?

My favorite sport is **tennis**.
What sport do you like best?

Well, what I like most is **swimming**.

cricket
⇨ soccer

volleyball
⇨ skiing

taekwondo
⇨ gymnastics

B. Listen and repeat the dialog. Then use the speaking cards to practice it with your partner.

⊙ Track **107**

A: Look at the club posters.

B: Wow! I want to join the ❶ ___Music Club___ .

A: Can you ❷ ___sing___ ?

B: Yes, I can.

A: I want to join the Extreme Sports Club.
 I want to learn how to ❸ ___snowboard___ .

B: Sounds interesting!

❶ Comedy Club

❷ tell jokes

❸ surf

❶ School Newspaper Club

❷ write stories

❸ scuba diving

Learn & Practice

- We use *how often* to ask about the **frequency of an action**. We use it generally with the present simple tense.

Q: **How often** do you brush your teeth?
A: (I brush my teeth) Three times a day.

How Often	Do/Does	Subject	Base Verb
How often	do	I/you/we/they	exercise?
	does	he/she/it	

- We use *can* to talk about **ability** in the present. To make **yes/no questions**, we put the helping verb *can* before the subject.

She **can** write with her left hand.

Q: **Can** she speak Korean?
A: Yes, she **can**. / No, she **can't**.

A. Complete the questions and answer them.

1. Q: _____How often do_____ you eat fast food?　　A: _____I usually eat fast food._____ (usually)

2. Q: _____ she exercise?　　A: _____ (twice a week)

3. Q: _____ they go to the gym?　　A: _____ (sometimes)

B. Make *yes/no* questions and complete the answers.

1. Yuri can speak English.　　Q: _Can Yuri speak English?_　　A: Yes, _she can_____.

2. It can float on water.　　Q: _____　　A: No, _____.

3. George can finish his work.　　Q: _____　　A: Yes, _____.

4. They can dance.　　Q: _____　　A: No, _____.

Super Speaking in Grammar

A. Listen to the conversation and practice with a partner. Use the cues given. Then change roles and practice again. Track 108

> How often does **she jog in the morning**?
>
> She jogs **three times a week** in the morning.

she / jog in the morning / ?
⇨ three times a week

they / walk to school / ?
⇨ five times a week

your dad / go canoeing / ?
⇨ once a month

Cindy / eat vegetables / ?
⇨ at least twice a day

B. Work with a partner. Ask questions and answer them. Use *Can you...*? Then ask *How about you*?

> Can Sophia speak Korean?

> No, she can't, but she can speak French. How about you?

> I can speak English. Your turn to ask!

Sophia

speak Korean / ?
No ⇨ French (O)

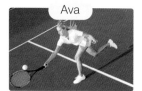

Ava

play soccer / ?
No ⇨ tennis (O)

Patricia

swim / ?
No ⇨ float on water(O)

Eric

snowboard / ?
No ⇨ skateboard (O)

they

play football / ?
No ⇨ basketball(O)

First Step in

English
Discussion

1
Answers

Iam books

Unit 01 Greetings

Getting Ready
A. 1. 3 2. 2 3. 4 4. 1

Building Vocabulary
A. 1. meet 2. name 3. bow 4. culture 5. prayers
6. respect

Super Activity!
A. my, Hi, I'm, meet, Nice, too
B. 1. the United States 2. Korea 3. China

Dialog
please call me, to meet, Where are you from, last name,
favorite subject, classmate

Answer the Questions
1. No, they aren't. 2. No, she isn't. 3. No, he isn't.
4. No, they aren't.

Language Focus!
A. 2. P: He is[He's] a singer. N: He is not[isn't] a singer.
3. P: We are[We're] nurses. N: We are not[aren't]
nurses.
B. 1. No, she isn't 2. Is, Yes, it is 3. Are, No, they aren't

Unit 02 Family

Getting Ready
A. 2. father - daughter 3. husband - wife
4. sister - brother 5. son - father 6. mother - daughter
B. Brian - 6, Lisa - 39, James - 42, Abigail - 11

Reading
A.

	Olivia	Chan	Mina
parents	2	2	2
brother	3	1	1
sister	2	1	
uncle	2		
aunt	3		
grandmother	1		
grandfather	1	1	

Building Vocabulary
A. 1. black eyes 2. grandfather 3. left-handed
4. uncle 5. sisters 6. family
B. Olivia - grandmother, Lisa - mother, Robert - uncle,
Joyce - aunt, Brian - younger brother, Elizabeth - cousin

Dialog
like your mother, left-handed, look like, salesman,
homemaker, photographer, black straight hair

Let's Talk
1. his mother 2. left-handed 3. a wildlife photographer

Language Focus!
A. 2. his 3. their
B. 2. boys' 3. Jane's 4. women's 5. My friend's
6. Peter's

Unit 03 Travel

Getting Ready
A. England - London - London Bridge - 1, USA - New York
- the Statue of Liberty - 5, China - Beijing - the Great
Wall - 3, Italy - Rome - the Colosseum - 2, Australia -
Sydney - the Sydney Opera House - 7, Egypt - Giza -
the Pyramids - 8, France - Paris - the Eiffel Tower - 6

Building Vocabulary
A. 1. beach 2. motorbike 3. sand 4. sea 5. world
6. suitcase

Super Activity!
A. 1. b 2. a 3. a 4. b

Dialog
package tour, absolutely, How many people, island, Would
you like to choose

Language Focus!
A. 2. are going to go 3. is going to study
4. is going to walk 5. are going to clean
6. are going to buy
B. 2. No, he isn't. He's going to buy a new cell phone
3. No, I'm not. I'm going to ride a horse

Unit 04 In My Free Time

Getting Ready
A. e, h, d, c, g, f, b, a

Building Vocabulary
A. surf the Internet - 5, read a book - 3, enjoy surfing - 6, do yoga - 7, go to the movies - 4, do taekwondo - 1, play soccer - 2, watch the international game - 8

Super Activity!
A. 1. 4   2. 3   3. 1   4. 2

Dialog
What do you do, How often, Saturday afternoon, play basketball, Do you play sports, how to play the guitar

Answer the Questions
1. No, he doesn't.
2. No, she doesn't.
3. He plays soccer once a week.

Language Focus!
A. 1. Do, b   2. Does, c   3. Does, a
B. 1. I sometimes take a shower.
　　2. She always jogs in the morning.
　　3. He is often late for school.

Unit 05 Food

Getting Ready
b - g - f - d - h - e - c - a

Building Vocabulary
A. 1. sandwiches   2. buy   3. various   4. different
　　5. traditional   6. meal

Super Activity!
A. 1. Sally - 2   2. Greg - 3   3. Amy - 1
B. 1. b   2. b   3. a

Dialog
ready to order, vegetable soup, What kind of, Would you like anything to drink, a bottle of

Answer the Questions
1. F   2. F   3. F   4. T

Language Focus!
A. 2. some   3. an   4. a   5. some   6. a
B. 2. a   3. some   4. an   5. a   6. some

Unit 06 Shopping

Getting Ready
c

Shopping and Prices
B. swimsuit - 7, sneakers - 5, T-shirt - 2, boots - 1, sun hat - 3, bag - 8, jeans - 6, socks - 4

Super Activity!
A. 1. Yes   2. No   3. No
B. 2. 75 cents   3. 5 cents   4. 25 cents   5. one dollar

Dialog
May I help you, Have you got, look very nice, a little small, a large, How much is it, too expensive, I'll take it

Answer the Questions
1. F   2. T   3. F   4. F

Super Discussion!
d, h, a, g, f, c, b

Language Focus!
A. 2. are waiting   3. is listening
B. 2. one   3. ones   4. one

Unit 07 Everyday Activities

Reading
· the country girl - Nancy
　the city girl - Judy

A. 1. 06:20   2. 05:35   3. 11:30   4. 03:00   5. 07:05
　　6. 04:45

Super Activity!

A. 2. He's, c 3. He's, b 4. They're, a 5. They're, d
6. They're, e

B. 1. c 2. c 3. a

Dialog

it's time for bed, favorite program, eight o'clock, nine thirty, ten o'clock, nine thirty, haven't got school

Language Focus!

A. 2. Q: Is she sitting on the chair? A: Yes, she is. / No, she isn't.

3. Q: Are Kevin and Lisa learning yoga? A: Yes, they are. / No, they aren't.

Unit 08 **Health**

Getting Ready

A. 2. John 3. Ann 4. Sophie 5. Lisa 6. Tina 7. Doug
8. Bill

Building Vocabulary

A. 1. vegetables 2. overweight 3. unhealthy 4. healthy
5. fried food 6. fast food

Super Activity!

A. 1. 2 2. 3 3. 4 4. 1

B. 1. a 2. b 2. a

Dialog

didn't come, a toothache, couldn't sleep, painkiller, pull it out, How do you feel now

Answer the Questions

1. F 2. T 3. T 4. F 5. T

Language Focus!

A. 2. shouldn't be 3. should take 4. shouldn't watch

Unit 09 **School Life**

Getting Ready

A. h, a, g, c, e, f, b, d

Building Vocabulary

A. 1. tired 2. school 3. lunchtime 4. different
5. geography 6. volleyball

Super Activity!

A. 1. b 2. a

B. 1. b 2. a

Dialog

school rules, must wear, can't eat, cell phone, have to, has to, really angry

Answer the Questions

1. F 2. T 3. F 4. T

Language Focus!

A. 2. You must stop. 3. You mustn't use your phone.
4. You must turn left.

B. 2. Can I turn on the TV?

Unit 10 **Special Days**

Getting Ready

C. 1. August 5th 2. April 3rd 3. May 15th

Building Vocabulary

A. 2. parents 3. a bow and arrow 4. yarn 5. general
6. stethoscope

Super Activity!

A. 1. a 2. b 3. b 4. b

B. 1. F 2. F 3. T

Dialog

celebrated, dress up, to collect, a treat, run out, wear costumes, an interesting custom

Language Focus!

A. 1. in 2. on 3. in 4. on 5. on 6. in

B. 2. to learn Korean 3. to see who it was
4. to study economics 5. to buy some books

Unit 11 My Dream Job

Getting Ready

A. 2. C 3. F 4. E 5. A 6. H 7. G 8. B 9. D

Building Vocabulary

A. 1. job 2. feel 3. famous 4. discover

Super Activity!

A. 3 - boring, 2 - dangerous, 1 - interesting

B. 1. b 2. a

Dialog

for a living, much fun, work, from, to, perfect job, don't like, far away, salesperson, customers, can, stressful

Answer the Questions

1. F 2. F 3. F

Language Focus!

2. Would you like 3. Olivia would like

4. They would like to go

Unit 12 Sports and Exercise

Getting Ready

A. e, h, a, g, c, d, f, b

Reading

A. 1. school cricket team 2. how to surf

3. surfing, a lot of fun

Building Vocabulary

A. 4. play basketball 5. do aerobics 6. play cricket

7. go surfing 8. do yoga

Super Activity!

A.

Name	What?	How often?
1. Ava	judo	three times a week
2. Peter	taekwondo	once a week
3. Ava's father	canoeing	once a month
4. Michelle	soccer	4 days a week

B. 1. b 2. a

Dialog

work out, fitness freak, how often, Do you play sports, what do you do, to change your life pattern

Answer the Questions

1. F 2. F 3. F 4. T

Language Focus!

A. 2. How often does, She exercises twice a week.

3. How often do, They sometimes go to the gym.

B. 2. Can it float on water?, it can't

3. Can George finish his work?, he can

4. Can they dance?, they can't